This portion of Robert Dixon's map of the appropriated lands of New South Wales in 1834 shows the location of Westwood, Hannibal Macarthur's property, where Joseph Mason spent most of his time as an assigned convict. To find Westwood place a straight edge beneath the words Port Hacking and look along the line to the west. The first property encountered is Westwood and Macarthur's name is printed obliquely beneath that of Wentworth.

JOSEPH MASON

JOSEPH MASON

ASSIGNED CONVICT, 1831–1837

'Doomed ... to the earth's remotest region'

Edited by David Kent & Norma Townsend
Introduction and Epilogue by David Kent

MELBOURNE UNIVERSITY PRESS

Melbourne University Press
PO Box 278, Carlton South, Victoria 3053, Australia

First published 1996

Designed by Sandra Nobes
Typeset by Syarikat Seng Teik Sdn. Bhd., Malaysia.
Printed in Malaysia by SRM Production Services Sdn. Bhd.

National Library of Australia Cataloguing-in-Publication entry

Mason, Joseph, 1799–1863.
Joseph Mason: assigned convict, 1831–1837.
ISBN 0 522 84746 3.
1. Mason, Joseph, 1799–1863. 2. Transportation of convicts—Australia. 3. Convicts—Australia—Biography. 4. Australia—History—1788–1851. I. Kent, David, 1942– . II. Townsend, Norma, 1941– . III. Title.
994.02092

Contents

Acknowledgements

IN 1995 I was able to spend several months in England researching for the book Norma Townsend and I are writing about the Swing protesters who were transported to New South Wales. The transcription of Joseph Mason's manuscript and the research for the Introduction were accomplished during that time and I thank the University of New England for granting me study leave. Norma Townsend and I acknowledge the help and encouragement provided by Dr Peter Durrant, County Archivist at the Berkshire Record Office where the Mason manuscript is held. His enthusiasm to see it made available to a wider audience prompted him to waive any claim to fees or royalties and we are grateful for his scholarly generosity. We also thank Miss Mollie Weedon of Cholsey in Oxfordshire, the owner of the manuscript, for graciously agreeing that it might be published.

David Kent

Armidale, NSW, 1996

Introduction

'Men of honest principle'

I

ON 26 JUNE 1831 the convict transport *Eleanor* anchored in Sydney Cove. Its unhappy human cargo consisted of 133 agricultural labourers and rural craftsmen who had been exiled for taking part in the protests which had swept across the English countryside late in the preceding year. The labouring men from Berkshire, Dorset, Hampshire and Wiltshire did not deserve their fate and it is doubtful if any convict vessel ever left England with a less criminal body of men aboard.

Among them was Joseph Mason, the author of the remarkable document reproduced in this volume, a gardener and labourer from the little village of Bullington in central Hampshire. The convict records list Mason's crime as machine-breaking, yet he broke no machines; he was tried and convicted for robbery, yet he robbed no-one. His real offence, for which he could not be openly charged, was that he was a radical, a critic of the *status quo* which condemned rural labourers in southern England to live in desperate poverty and kept them politically powerless to alter their circumstances. Joseph's younger brother, Robert, who was also transported to New South Wales, was entirely correct when he wrote to a fellow villager that they were banished 'because we advocated the cause of him who lived in a land of plenty, yet never knew what it was to have enough'. The Masons undoubtedly played a prominent role in organising the labourers' protest in their locality, but they were convicted of trumped-up offences in order that the nation might be safe from dangerous men who dared to demand that working people be fairly treated.

During the winter of 1830–31 much of southern, central and eastern England was shaken by the upheaval of rural discontent, the product of long-endured poverty and hunger. From the 1790s, the processes of agrarian capitalism had made the rural labourer a pauper. By 1830, most adult labourers had only ever known an existence of inadequate wages, supplemented by barely adequate poor relief, combined with regular underemployment and periodic unemployment. This kept them and their families in constant poverty and often on the brink of starvation. The labourers wanted little from life beyond a living wage and the opportunity to earn it, but even these most basic expectations were increasingly difficult to realise.

In a little over a generation, the agricultural labourer in southern England had become a pauper, but the men and their families who suffered this remorseless impoverishment were never wholly crushed by the process. Protest, after all, is rarely the action of people who are content to be victims but is a course adopted by those who believe they have been wronged, who sense that they can help themselves and are resolved to set things right. The labourers' goals were simple: they wanted better wages and regularity of employment. To achieve those ends in 1830, they employed a range of very traditional tactics.

The disturbances of 1830–31 are usually remembered for the wholesale destruction of threshing machines. This labour-displacing innovation was greatly resented by agricultural labourers; hand-threshing, using the flail, provided one of the few remaining opportunities for work in the wintertime. The use of threshing machines had been one of the major grievances of the East Anglian labourers during the disturbances of 1816 and 1822. In the autumn and early winter of 1830, many machines were destroyed across southern England. Machine-breaking, however, was not the only form of protest. Incendiary attacks, public meetings to negotiate better wages and poor law allowances, and threatening letters signed by the mythical 'Captain Swing', were all used in a barrage of persuasion intended to prompt farmers and landowners to raise wages, preserve employment and fulfil their customary responsibilities. The disturbances, which began in Kent and swept through more than twenty counties in three months, reached Hampshire in mid-November. Open agitation commenced on 17 November and lasted for barely a week but so widespread was the upheaval that the county was, with Wiltshire, the most troubled in England.

In a typical incident, a crowd of men visited the farms and substantial houses of their locality to destroy agricultural machines where they found them, secure agreement that wages would rise, usually to two shillings a day, and solicit donations of food, drink and money. The visits were generally disciplined and surprisingly courteous. In many respects the labourers' behaviour was little different from those other occasions in the rural calendar when customary collective begging provided a valuable supplement to household income and diet. Many confrontations took place in daylight between men who knew each other, so that the participants were easily identified and subsequently prosecuted. The labourers protested openly and boldly because they were convinced that their actions were legitimate and they placed their trust in direct action which was a customary method of focusing attention on social grievances.

Machine-breaking was not anarchic; it was part of workplace culture in many occupations and a long-established strategy by which working people protected their interests. By destroying the hated threshing machines, the labourers preserved an important opportunity for winter work. They also displayed their hostility to a device which was a symbol of the socially destructive farming practices that had made them paupers. Without consciously realising it, the labourers were making a last stand for the community-based values of the pre-industrial world, already substantially eroded by the seductive new morality of individualism and self-interest.

In the aftermath of the disturbances the aristocratic state exacted a terrible and terrifying retribution. In Hampshire alone, almost 300 men were tried before a Special Commission whose purpose was to make an example of them and deter on-going protest elsewhere. Over 100 were sentenced to death. Three were executed and 117 transported to New South Wales or Van Diemen's Land. Protesters were transported from twenty-one counties but those from Hampshire accounted for almost a quarter of those so sentenced. More were transported for their part in the agricultural disturbances than for all the other protests which troubled the Engish authorities between 1790 and 1848.

Transportation had a profound psychological effect on the communities of those exiled and the ruling elite relied on its terrifying example. For an equivalent use of the terror of transportation, one must look to the aftermath of Culloden in 1745 and the Irish revolt in 1798. England had seen nothing to rival the punishments handed down after the Swing disturbances since Monmouth's rebellion almost 150 years previously. Unlike those events, which challenged the political establishment and involved the prospect of civil war, the agricultural disturbances were essentially a 'bread and cheese affair'. The protesters were, as Joseph Mason noted, 'men of honest principle' who had been driven beyond the point of passive acceptance and had courageously asserted their claim to fair treatment. Unfortunately for them, the disturbances alarmed the landowning class whose paranoia caused it to see any large-scale protest as a possible prelude to revolution. The protests were, therefore, repressed by a chillingly deliberate application of legal terror and many men were 'doomed to cross the ocean to the earth's remotest region'.

II

JOSEPH MASON WAS not a typical agricultural labourer in three respects; he had the use of some land, he was highly literate and he was politically active. Joseph, with Robert, rented a small-holding of 3½ acres which gave the brothers a modicum of independence. Although they also worked as farm labourers, their little piece of ground allowed them to keep a cow, grow some vegetables and sometimes fatten a pig. The household, which also contained their mother and Joseph's wife and infant daughter, was never as impoverished as many around them. As a result, the brothers were somewhat less dependent on the local farmers for employment and they never required poor relief. This alone made them unusual and quite possibly explains why their less fortunate fellow labourers regarded them as community leaders.

The family had arrived in Bullington sometime before 1820 after periods in Hurstbourne Tarrant, where Joseph was born in 1799, and Martyr Worthy, the birthplace of Robert in 1805. The brothers' father was a gardener whose death in 1820 left the family in straitened circumstances. This may well have caused Joseph to return home from his position as servant to a Mr Fitzwater at Cranbourne near Windsor. Joseph's principal duties consisted of driving his master about in a gig and performing athletic feats at Fitzwater's request. According to Robert, the latter 'was often making bets on my brother of running or leaping . . . no gate, no hedge, no style was too high for him; he would clear all like a Kangaroo and could run a mile in 4 minutes and 40 seconds'. While employed by Fitzwater, Joseph met Ann Champ whom he married several years later in 1829.

By the late 1820s, the family was better placed than most and enjoyed a modest existence derived from its collective endeavour. The brothers earned wages when they could and tended their land. Their mother kept a dame school for a handful of pupils and two sisters were comfortably placed in domestic service. The brothers, however, would suffer for their hard work; their position above the common rank of labourers was held against them at their trials as were their education and political views.

Joseph and Robert were both fully literate; that is, they could read *and* write. Their parents were similarly literate and the brothers acquired all their schooling at home. Although Joseph claimed to be 'quite unacquainted with the true art of writing' and to 'know nothing of grammar', he grew sufficiently confident later in his life to write at least one tract to his fellow parishioners about the Romish practices introduced by their vicar; Robert had an article on the misuse of colonial government funds published in the *Maitland Mercury*. In 1863 Joseph commented on his lack of formal education in verse:

> *No lectures I ever heard read*
> *The barn was my school or the garden or field*
> *And instead of the pen it was the flail I must wield*
> *Or the scythe or the hoe or the spade*

He penned topical, moralising and even humorous verse in his letters to friends and family; on matters of great meaning to him he thundered like an Old Testament prophet. While a surprisingly high proportion of agricultural labourers could read, Joseph and Robert were unusual among their fellows in being able to write and exceptionally rare in the sophistication of their literacy.

It is evident from the brothers' letters that, like so many other working-class literates in the early nineteenth century, these deeply religious men had read and absorbed much from the Bible. It is probable that they also knew many of the other classic texts such as *Pilgrim's Progress*. There are enough references in Joseph's account of his time in New South Wales to show that he read voraciously the limited material which came his way. To the end of his life he continued his pursuit of knowledge in that relentless manner peculiar to the autodidact. His letters are full of information culled from newspapers and journals which he enthusiastically passed on to his correspondents in Australia and he devoured the colonial papers sent to him. Joseph was always a questioning and reflective reader and it was probably as a result of this process that Robert and he became political radicals.

The brothers were members of the Radical and Musical Society which met at the White Swan tavern in Sutton Scotney. The society's name accurately reflected the manner in which the members began their meetings—with some beer and a song—before proceeding to a discussion of political issues raised by the latest copy of Cobbett's *Political Register*. Radicalism flourished where people had access to ideas and opportunities to discuss them in a reasonably free social environment. In 'open' villages like Sutton, where the influence of the squire and parson was less significant and tradesmen more numerous, radical ideas and religious Dissent took root more easily than in 'closed' villages like nearby Micheldever which Sir Thomas Baring controlled tightly. According to a local magistrate the artisans and craftsmen in places like Sutton were 'universally politicians'. The Radical and Musical Society included among its members shopkeepers, shoemakers, sawyers and butchers, as well as small farmers and agricultural labourers.

Sutton was the largest of the villages along the road beside the tiny River Dever which flowed into the River Test at Chilbolton. With Wonston, Stoke Charity and Micheldever to the east and Bullington, Barton Stacey and Chilbolton to the west, Sutton was the natural centre of a valley that is only 9 miles long. It straddled the London road and was a conduit for news of all sorts as carriers brought pamphlets, letters, newspapers, gossip and radical ideas into the area. In 1831 the Attorney-General complained that the *Political Register* had a 'prodigious effect' on working people who often clubbed together 'in great societies' to buy copies which were read 'in many places where the poor are in the habit of resorting'. This was exactly what happened in Sutton where the members of the Society resolved at a meeting on 29 September 1830 that they would compose a petition to the King.

The petition, drawn up by Joseph Mason, was prompted by Cobbett's 'Letter to the King' published in the *Political Register* ten days previously. The tone and structure of the petition owed much to Cobbett, but Joseph thoughtfully incorporated local details to reflect the Society's concerns. The petitioners claimed that the 'misery and distress' endured by the 'working and labouring classes' was the direct consequence of the people's lack of representation in a Parliament filled with men 'in whom the people have no confidence'. Governments, it was suggested, existed to regulate civil society 'to protect the weak against the strong . . . the poor against the unjust encroachments of the rich . . . [and] protect the welfare and happiness of the people'. It was clear to the Mason brothers and the other 174 men—mostly agricultural labourers from Bullington, Wonston and Barton Stacey—who endorsed the document by signature or mark that the government was failing in its basic duties. His Majesty was informed that at Barton Stacey a man with a wife and three children was expected to live on eight shillings a week, 'out of which we have to pay, one shilling for the rent of our house, and one for fuel' so that the family had to exist on ten pence a day. It was claimed that 'many of us have not food sufficient to satisfy our hunger' and that clothes and fuel were in equally short supply, while the government placed heavy taxes on the 'necessaries of the poor man's life'.

The petitioners had a catalogue of social and political grievances: the pensions and sinecures 'wantonly heaped on the . . . aristocracy', the maintenance of an army in peacetime 'fed and clothed out of the fruit of our labour', the tithes paid to 'rich men in the church', the use of summary justice and the game laws which punished the poor for taking 'for our own use the wild birds and animals . . . those things being kept for the support of the rich'. The only remedy was a reform of the political system based on '*annual Parliaments, universal suffrage*, and *vote by ballot*'. Until that was achieved, the petitioners declared, working people could not expect to enjoy their 'hard-earned little'.

The Sutton Scotney petition was uncompromising in its social and political radicalism and shows how wrong it is to assume that rural workers were indifferent to political matters. Almost all the adult men in Bullington signed the document which Joseph carried on foot to the royal residence in Brighton, some 60 miles away. Members of the Society raised money for his expenses on the journey by subscribing a few pence each, but their self-sacrifice was wasted. Even though Joseph pestered the royal servants, he was refused permission to deliver the petition and told to take it to the Home Department in London. Unable to afford the time or the money to extend his journey by another 120 miles, Joseph gave the petition to an acquaintance in Brighton who, in turn, passed it on until eventually it came into Cobbett's hands.

The Times scornfully dismissed Joseph and the other village radicals who petitioned the King in the name of the 'sovereign people' as 'Hampshire bumpkins', but in November 1830 those 'bumpkins' organised and directed the largest rural protest in the county. As readers of the *Political Register* they might even have expected upheaval. From the mid-1820s Cobbett had been predicting a rural revolt and in 1829 he suggested that the poor had only themselves to blame if, as starvation stalked the land, 'they *lie down like dogs* and die with hunger'. On 13 November, less than a week before the disturbances began around Sutton,

Joseph attended another meeting at the White Swan. Only ten people were present and it is possible that the strategy of strikes and machine-breaking which began on 19 November was planned that night—although it was later claimed that the meeting was to plan another petition. A couple of nights later, some labourers met at a house in Sutton where Joseph read a letter which

> said we was all to leave off work; and the Sutton men was to go out and stop the ploughs. They was to send home the horses for the farmers to look after themselves, and was to take the men with them. And they was to go and turn the men out of the barns. And they was all to go and break the 'sheens' as the farmers had got to do the thrashing.

It is probable that similiar instructions were issued to groups in the other villages for on 19 November protest action began simultaneously along the length of the Dever Valley.

III

BETWEEN 800 AND 1000 labourers took part in the protest. Several crowds moved up and down the valley during the day before finally congregating at Sutton in the evening. The labourers' aspirations were simple; they told the curate of Stoke Charity, Reverend Cockerton, that 'the only thing they wanted to do was to break the machinery'. He resisted the men's request for a donation and tried to dissuade them from their course.

Although he received a polite hearing, the men were not diverted. They refused to disband and asked him to go to Sutton and put their case to the farmers 'for you can do it better than us'.

An hour or so later, a crowd of around 100 arrived at Borough Farm, Micheldever, where they informed William Paine that 'they wanted an advance of wages to 2s a day, and to break his machinery'. Paine readily agreed to pay the higher wage, sealing his promise with a gift of beer, but he tried to preserve his threshing machine. The young men in the crowd, however, were adamant that it had to be destroyed. Their wages were already well below those of the married men and they had more to lose if machine-threshing continued. A member of the Radical and Musical Society later claimed that the young men were chiefly responsible for the disturbances in the Dever Valley for they 'led the others and forced them into it'.

Joseph and Robert Mason always maintained that they had been compelled to go along with the crowd on 19 November. According to Robert, the men who came to their garden in Bullington threatened them with 'a warm bed or a warm death'. If the brothers were, indeed, unwillingly co-opted it is probable that they were enlisted because of their reputation as articulate, politically aware individuals. It is understandable that the younger men, intent on forceful action which had evidently been planned beforehand, might have looked to the Masons for leadership. However, it would be unwise to place too much emphasis on the brothers' defence that they were press-ganged, for all the evidence points to their having a less involuntary role in the organisation of the protest. Joseph, it will be recalled, had announced the strategy of strikes and machine-breaking to a group in Sutton just a few days previously and throughout the days' events the brothers were at the centre of the crowd, directing and controlling its actions but scrupulously refraining from taking direct action themselves.

The crowds visited farmers up and down the valley, destroying machinery and collecting money as a reward for their service. William Paine and Richard Deare were charged £1. Thomas Dowden was asked to pay twice that amount 'because he had most land' while £10 was levied from Francis Callendar, the steward of Sir Thomas Baring's large estate. Contributions were also demanded from those whose wealth and position made them targets of social resentment. Robert Mason was with a party which requested food, drink and money from the Reverend James Joliffe of Barton Stacey. The clergyman refused, pleading poverty, but his remarks sounded hollow to the men at his gate. As someone said, 'you have it and we want it, we have been living upon potatoes long enough and now we must have something better'.

Given the number of self-professed radicals in the crowd, it is possible that the graduated impost and the donations demanded from the prosperous and propertied were seen as a tax on wealth. Notions of social justice and equitable taxation were an important element in the labourers' petition and radical political views were frequently heard during the protest. Sir Thomas Baring complained that his labourers in Stratton and Micheldever told him 'we are going to have another constitution—the heads have been in power long enough and now it is our turn'.

Although some labourers used menacing language, the protest on 19 November was neither a rebellion nor a frenzied *jacquerie*. There was little violence and almost no unnecessary damage because the radical leadership kept a tight control over the crowd's behaviour. Francis Callendar extracted a pledge, probably from Joseph Mason, that the crowd would avoid the Baring mansion, Stratton House, if Callendar donated £10. The promise was kept and the crowd was followed to a public house by Callendar's clerk. The men were treated to half a pint of beer each; there was no orgy of drunkenness. The clerk was instructed to keep a record of the beer drawn and was given £5 by Joseph to settle the bill. Later, the men mustered in a meadow where he distributed the balance of the money collected during the day.

The protest ended at Sutton in the early evening with an outcome the labourers could not have expected twelve hours previously. A local magistrate confronted the crowd, listened to its grievances and agreed that he would propose to the farmers a wage increase to twelve shillings a week for married men and nine shillings for the unmarried together with an increase in the scales of poor relief. On the strength of this promise the labourers went back to work the next day. Their protest had been successful.

While the political agenda of the Dever Valley radicals was forward-looking in many respects, the form of their protest belonged to an older world of custom and community.

Firstly, the crowds did not venture beyond the group of parishes in which they lived and worked. Grievances were traditionally resolved and charity sought within the community because the labourers' confidence in a social code based on mutual aid and collective well-being presumed that masters and men, donors and recipients knew each other intimately. Secondly, in their perambulation around the valley farms the protesters followed another long-established practice. Processioning, on many different occasions, was an important aspect of village life which reinforced the geographical and social boundaries of the community. Thirdly, the collection of donations of food, drink and money was in keeping with many other events in the rural calendar. On those occasions the poor demanded charity from the prosperous members of the community and the menace of personal humiliation or damage to property was part of the customary proceedings.

Plough bullocks, shrovers, mummers, wassailers and others expected their efforts to be rewarded with a donation which was regarded as a payment for a service performed. In this way the recipients of rural charity preserved their dignity and did not see themselves as beggars. Sharing food and drink was also a time-honoured way of sealing arrangements, celebrating the cycle of rural tasks and cementing social relations in the countryside. The labourers saw the largesse they solicited on 19 November as their reward for saving the community from the socially destructive consequences of machine-threshing and, therefore, as an endorsement of their actions.

The labourers believed that the menace which usually accompanied collective begging did not compromise the legitimacy of the demand; provided the donation was given, and not actually taken by force, they remained within the law. A Micheldever man defended himself against a charge of robbery by insisting that he only asked 'civilly for the money' which the farmer gave him 'and that he thanked him very kindly for it'. The law, however, declared Justice Alderson, recognised no such evasion; if menace was implied, it was immaterial how the money was received. Taking it was a felony. By admitting his involvement with collective begging that labourer exposed himself to a capital charge. Behaviour which was customarily associated with collective begging in its various forms was, on this occasion, seen as evidence of criminal conduct. It was a complete betrayal of customary practice. Custom shaped the labourers' protest and underpinned their claim to fair treatment. It gave them a repertoire of performance, it allowed them to believe that their actions were legitimate and it explains the self-confidence of their protest. For these reasons they were unprepared for the punishment which sent men to Australia for behaviour they did not consider criminal.

IV

THE FIRST OF the Special Commissions established to try the rural protesters met at Winchester a few days before Christmas.

The Duke of Wellington, Lord Lieutenant of Hampshire, had pressed the idea of a Special Commission on the new Whig government in the hope that it would 'tranquilize' not only the county but 'the Country in general'. The government, faced with the spread of disturbances to East Anglia and the Midlands, resolved to deal with the Hampshire prisoners in a manner which displayed its readiness to crush protest anywhere. Lord Melbourne at the Home Department was also concerned that local magistrates might deal too leniently with the labourers if the trials were left in their jurisdiction. Many magistrates had authorised wage increases and had thus implicitly confirmed the legitimacy of the labourers' cause. By using Special Commissions the government was able to apply a policy of maximum severity uncompromised by local considerations.

The Crown went to extraordinary lengths to secure a conviction against the Masons and the other village radicals. According to Baron Vaughan, one of the Commissioners, the disturbances in the Dever Valley were 'instigated by the suggestions of evil designing persons'. He had in mind the Masons, 'men in the occupation of land and gardeners' who had incited 'tumult and riot'. The Attorney-General, who directed the case against the brothers, drew the jury's attention to 'their superior education and intelligence' and argued that their status above mere labourers made their offence far more serious. Robert's effort to prompt the villagers of some neighbouring parishes into petitioning the King as the meeting at Sutton had done was already known to the Home Department. Captain John

Thompson informed Melbourne that the brothers 'for months past . . . have been actively employed in sowing the seeds of disaffection'. He maintained that he could trace their progress through Longparish from house to house and 'fix them at one of the new beer houses with an assemblage of persons of different ranks . . . listening to speeches and signing a petition to the King'. The Masons were clearly marked down for special attention.

The brothers, in company with others, were indicted for 'robbing' Francis Callendar of £10. Six of the eight men charged had signed the Sutton petition. It was proved that the Masons were in the crowd but it was not claimed that they had asked for or received money, or taken part in any machine-breaking. They were acquitted, with four others, on this count but were then charged with 'robbing' Thomas Dowden. Six of the twelve men indicted for this offence were Sutton petitioners. Again it was demonstrated that Joseph had been part of the crowd, but nothing more serious could be proved against him. This time, however, he was convicted because the Commissioners decreed that a felony committed by one person in a crowd made everyone present liable to the legal penalty (irrespective of their proximity to the event or the unwillingness of their participation). In sentencing Joseph, Baron Vaughan declared that he was to 'suffer the severest penalty of the law' for the conspicuous part he played in the events of 19 November. As a 'person moving in a better condition of life' he had no business being involved with the labourers' protest and he was, therefore, to be 'cut off from all communication with society and transported for life'.

Robert Mason, acquitted of 'robbing' Thomas Dowden because his presence could not be proved, was then charged with 'robbing' Reverend Joliffe who had given five shillings to the crowd. He felt the injustice of the prosecution very bitterly and wrote to Joliffe from Winchester Gaol; 'five shillings could not have been a great loss to you—there were not the least injury done or threatened to your person or property, nor a saucy or disrespectful word uttered as I heard, you was thanked for your donation'. All that could be proved against Robert was that he had been part of the crowd which called on Joliffe and had been seen carrying a stick. Although Joliffe admitted that he had known Robert for years, that he had attended Joliffe's church, that he had never done a dishonest deed or committed a breach of the peace, it was all to no avail. In his letter to Joliffe, Robert concluded that he had been indicted 'because my political opinions differed from your own' and he alluded to evidence of a conspiracy among the witnesses who had agreed in advance what each had to say in order to obtain a conviction. At the third attempt this village radical was convicted of 'robbery' under the all-encompassing interpretation of the law used by the Commissioners.

Even after the trials were concluded, the authorities still looked for evidence which would fix responsibility for the protests on the Masons. The brothers were known to have read the *Political Register* to their fellow villagers at Bullington; this alone identified them as dangerous men to a government deeply suspicious of popular radicalism and opposed to the notion that labouring men might be entitled to the vote. Unsuccessful attempts were made to elicit confessions from the men in Winchester Gaol that they had been prompted to engage in the protest because of their familiarity with the writings of Cobbett. One of the Sutton petitioners recalled how he was approached 'times and times' in gaol by a clerical visitor who offered him immunity 'if I would only tell what I knowed' about the Masons. He was made to watch the execution of two prisoners in an attempt, he said, 'to frighten us by it to tell all we knowed . . . Had I told what I knowed, they'd ha' been hung . . . but I wouldn't split'. So the brothers' death sentences were commuted to transportation for life and, with forty-seven other Hampshire men, they were exiled to New South Wales.

The Masons fully understood the undeclared reason for their banishment and, confident of their innocence, they remained incorrigibly defiant. Robert wrote to his friends in Bullington urging them 'not to be cast down and trod under for ever more for what have happened'. He instructed a fellow radical to prepare a petition for the return of the exiles 'as there must be a reformed Parliament or a Revolution before next summer'. From New South Wales the brothers kept up an irregular correspondence with the radical network at home and it was a subscription raised by the brothers' friends and sympathisers which, in 1837, paid for Joseph's fare home. Charles Bastin of Wherwell, to whom Joseph addressed his account of his time in the colony, appears to have been a shoemaker and was almost certainly a fellow radical. It is likely that he had been a neighbour in

Bullington in the 1820s and the families were certainly close because a Maria Bastin attended Joseph's funeral. Bastin may well have been instrumental in organising the subscription which brought Joseph home. If that was indeed the case, then it is likely that Joseph's account was written as an expression of gratitude.

V

JOSEPH MASON'S TIME in New South Wales needs no discussion here, for his story is set out in the ensuing pages and to summarise his memoir would spoil the pleasures of discovery which await the reader. There is much in his narrative to interest the historian apart from the specific events and the topics he wrote about. In particular, it provides an unusual insight into the living and working experiences of convicts under assignment. Perhaps the most obvious, but possibly unexpected, feature to emerge from Joseph's account is the degree of liberty, within certain limits, which some convicts under sentence might enjoy.

Joseph's is a highly reliable story of his experiences in the colony, devoid of the exaggeration, hyperbole and self-justification found in so many other published contemporary memoirs. His account of his explorations along the Nepean River through what is known today as the Bents Basin Nature Reserve is a masterpiece of description which captures the dramatic landscape of the gorge so accurately that it might serve as a guide for the modern bushwalker. Joseph probably kept a diary or journal while he was in New South Wales, for his narrative often contains very precise details of time, place and event which were unlikely to have been remembered without some form of record. He was also scrupulously honest in declaring where his observations or comments were not based on personal experience but were the product of hearsay or reading.

Joseph's account should be read as a private communication between friends. Its purpose was to give Charles Bastin, a man familiar with the agriculture and landform of the Hampshire chalklands, some understanding of the alien environment into which the exiles had been cast. Joseph wrote about topics which were the familiar conversational fare of English countrymen. He commented on the settlements and buildings he had seen, on gardening and farming in New South Wales, and on the landscape with its birds, beasts and reptiles. Knowing only the intensively cultivated and orderly fields of southern England, Joseph was acutely aware of the very foreign character of the wilderness landscape which surrounded him on the Nepean River.

The property where he served his sentence was, in 1831, on the frontier of settlement to the east of the Blue Mountains. Although a road over the mountains gave access to the interior, the eastern foothills were still largely unexplored and unsurveyed. Little land had been cleared for cultivation and most of the grazing properties were still densely forested. Comparisons with the benign climate and gentle, enclosed countryside of Hampshire were inevitable yet Joseph, unusually for his time, saw the Australian bush as different but not inferior. A sense of wonder pervades his descriptions of its pristine grandeur and vastness of scale; he was in awe of the natural elements which seemed so much more powerful and savage than anything he had known in England. Joseph was also more fair-minded and tolerant in his depiction of the Aborigines he encountered than were many of his contemporaries. He shared some Eurocentric prejudices, it is true, but he was at pains to condemn the mistreatment of Aborigines and to praise some of their obvious accomplishments. But however well he wrote, Joseph believed he could not do his subject justice; he assured Bastin that no-one could imagine Australia using a repertoire of English images and experiences. The land and its indigenous people were *sui generis*.

Joseph was granted an absolute pardon in July 1836, although he did not receive news of his liberty for a further four months. As a free man he was able to visit Robert whom he had not seen for five and a half years. In January 1837 he took a steamer to Newcastle and on up the Hunter River to the Williams River and the property where his brother was assigned. The news that all the rural protesters of 1830 were to be pardoned had circulated throughout the colony and one can imagine the joy of the brothers' reunion and the excitement with which they laid their plans to return home. They could not go back together because Robert's conditional pardon was not approved until November 1837 but they parted on 10 January 1837 believing that in a year they would be together 'on the soil that gave us birth'. They never met again.

David Kent

Editorial Note

JOSEPH MASON'S MANUSCRIPT consists of 114 closely written pages and almost 46 000 words written in two distinct hands. In preparing the transcription for publication we have restricted our editorial activity to instances where our intrusion will, we hope, aid the reader and we have clearly indicated all such occasions by the use of square brackets [ ]. In some places we felt it was necessary to construct several sentences where Mason used a single rambling one, and these are identified by bracketed capital letters. Where the writer has obviously used the wrong word or has used a spelling which is not immediately clear, we have supplied an alternative meaning or the correct spelling in the same font as the text. Where a word is omitted without a clear break in the text we have inserted a likely choice in [*italic type*] and we have indicated by [*word missing*] the gaps in the manucript. The few words which we have been unable to decipher are indicated by a question mark. We have retained the erratic punctuation of the original text and have not attempted to punctuate it for modern readers. We hope these editorial decisions make the text more accessible and are confident that they in no way affect its tone or style.

David Kent

Norma Townsend

Note on Conversion

Joseph Mason used the old British Imperial currency and units of measurement. Their modern metric equivalents are shown below.

currency

12d (12 pence)	=	1/–, 1s (1 shilling)	=	10 cents
20s (20 shillings)	=	£1 (1 pound)	=	$2.00
21s = £1.1s	=	1 guinea	=	$2.10

weight

		1 pound	=	0.4 kilograms
14 pounds	=	1 stone	=	6.4 kilograms
8 stone	=	1 hundredweight	=	50.9 kilograms
20 hundredweight	=	1 ton	=	1.02 tonnes

length

		1 inch	=	25.4 millimetres
12 inches	=	1 foot	=	30.5 centimetres
3 feet	=	1 yard	=	91.4 centimetres
22 yards	=	1 chain	=	20.1 metres
10 chains	=	1 furlong	=	201.2 metres
8 furlongs	=	1 mile	=	1.6 kilometres

area

4840 square yards	=	1 acre	=	0.4 hectares
640 acres	=	1 square mile	=	259 hectares

volume

		1 pint	=	0.5 litres
8 pints	=	1 gallon	=	3.7 litres
8 gallons	=	1 bushel	=	30 litres

THE MEMOIR

1838
To Charles Bastin of Wherwell Hants

HAVING WHILE AN exile at the Antipodes addressed a letter to you with which you expressed yourself much Interested and having since through the assistance of kind friends under the guidance and superintendence of a beneficient and merciful Providence been blessed with a restoration to my native land—Having now circumnavigated the globe and been in the four quarters of the world—Having with feelings as much at variance as the scenery is anomalous traversed the streets of the seat of empire and climed the mountains of the dreary wilderness—Having seen the centre and summit of civilization and nature in all her rusticity simplicity beauty and deformity and being now after an absence of seven years again seated by an English fireside and enjoying the society of those I love and revere I propose with the permission of Him who has been my guardian protector to write for your perusal a sketch of what has fallen within my observation during the period of our separation while I remain what I was prior to that separation

Your sincere and wellwishing friend Josh Mason.

The Memoir

BORN AS I WAS of parents too poor to bestow on me a liberal education and bred up in a small sequestered village of farm labourers where there was not a single mechanic shut out in a manner from society and the world with no other means of cultivating the understanding or improving the mind but such as a bountiful providence has been pleased to bestow on Self application you may not look for beauty of Speech or eloquence of language but which is preferable in my opinion I will vouch for the Authenticity of the narrative and you may therefore depend on it as such.

With regards to the disturbance which pervaded the south of England in the year 1830 for which I was banished the land of my birth and my dearest friends I shall say but little yet a veneration for that divine attribute Truth as well as a vindication of my own cause compels me to state that whatever may have been the opinion of some persons on the subject nothing of the sort was meditated by me nor did a word of advice for such a proceeding ever escape my lips. And I say now as I did at the special commission that the statement of one of the witnesses (and that a material one) was as far from truth as it is possible for one object to be from another. But you know that myself with hundreds besides was doomed to cross the ocean to the earths remotest region. The ship in which I went conveyed 133 and we sailed from Portsmouth on Saturday evening of the 19th of Feb[y.] 1831 we crossed the Equator on the 22nd. of March and arrived at the Cape of Good Hope April 27th..[1] We anchored in Simons close enough to the town to read the names over the shop doors[2] We were not permitted to go on shore but from the ship the town appeared very neat and clean it lays close to the sea at the foot of a range of lofty barren mountains the rugged rocks at the summit of which appear as if ready to tumble down and crush the houses to pieces The walls of the buildings are mostly white and the doors and window shutters painted green so that it looks lively and gay [D]uring the 6 days we stayed we saw the coaches go out and come into the town every morning [*and*] evening some of them we traced with the eye a good way along the beach and others we soon lost sight of as they turned suddenly round the rocks and disapeared among the mountains Carts Wagons &c are drawn chiefly by oxen and we saw as many as 12 or 14 in a teams at times Altogether they [there] seemed a considerable deal of business going on and a Motley mixture of people by whom it is transacted they are partly Dutch Portugese & French though it is now an English Settlement and their features display almost every shade from the jet black Hottentot to the fair English lady Great numbers of the Hottentots are employed in rowing boats in the

Harbour all of whom wore hats without brims and in shape and substance as much like salt baskets as if they were actually such [O]n Sunday I observed that the Carpenters sawyers blacksmiths and the like went to work the same as on other days but on the chiming of the bells about 10 oclock they all left their work and hastened to [*church*] and when the service was over many of them resumed their tasks but judging from appearances I should Imagine not from compulsion [T]he burial ground is ½ a mile or more out of the town and a funeral which took place during our stay was conducted in a very different manner to what we see them in England [T]he corpse was carried in something resembling a handbarrow and in the rear of the mourners if such they may be termed instead of in the front A good many persons proceeded to the place of interment who as soon as the corpse was let into the ground scampered off in various directions towards the town as if vying with each other in which should reach home first The bay is large I should think 12 or 14 miles across and though the entrance is wide it cannot be seen from a ship laying near the town and the appearance is that of a large basin of water completely surrounded by mountains far below whose summits we frequently saw the clouds roll along [W]e were told by persons who came on board that the land in the interior was rich but the appearance while in the harbour and along the coast as far as we sailed and as far as the eye could reach is just the reverse of fertility nothing but mountains without a tree and but half covered with grass and a small plant which looked something like heath is to be seen Myself and a few others were much amused while in the harbour every morning at sunrise in listening to the report and echo of a gun from a man of war ship The sound seemed to go from the ship and strike hard against the sides of the rocks on shore from which it recoiled with a power little less than it preceeded with But part of the sound missed the first rocks and entered the deep narrow chasms that in many places divide the mountains in which confined situation it made a long rumbling noise like thunder Whether it escaped from one of these ravines and then entered another or whether the original report from the ship entered several chasms some of which were longer than others in conveying the sound back to us I cannot say but when it had subsided in one place and as we at first thought had come to a close it commenced afresh and with equal strength in a different and almost opposite direction and this was repeated several times and each time in a different place. We took in some sheep at this place which are of a very peculiar kind they are of a light brown colour and their covering is a mixture of wool and hair [T]hey are thin and small about the neck and shoulders and their chief substance is in the hindquarter but more particularly in the tail which is as thick as the calf of a mans leg and is a solid lump of fat weighing from 6 to 10 lbs. it is not more than 8 or 9 inches in length and hangs down straight with a small top turning up about as large as ones little finger These sheep with a good goat and her kid some fresh water and fuel comprised the stock we took in and which occupied 5 working days this with one Sunday made our stay 6 days in the evening of the last of which the anchor was got up and we made another start but for want of sufficient wind we could not get out of the bay before Midnight The same want of wind continued throughout the whole of the following day & at the close of evening we were still within sight of land nor did we gain much ground on the three following days but on the Friday about daylight a very powerful gale of wind commenced which continued three days & the sea became so agitated that the waves came over the bulwarks and put out the fire every time an attempt was made to light one so that we could get no victuals cooked and were therefore obliged to live on dry biscuit and this occured another three days at a subsequent period before we arrived at Sydney The Cape of good hope and Sydney lays in the same parallel of latitude that is between 33 and 34 degrees south of the Equator but few if any captains of ships in the present day attempt to run in a straight line on account of the variable winds which prevail in that latitude while from the 46th to the 50th parallel there is an almost constant current of wind from the west all the year round[3] [O]ur captain made his way to this latitude & we had very strong winds at times which we also felt very cold it being the southern winter About half way between the cape & Sydney there are two Islands called Amsterdam & St Pauls known also by the name of the Islands of Desolation between which we passed with a good view of both and saw land no more till we entered Bass Straits which divide New South Wales and Van Diemens Land. We arrived in these Straits on the 19 June and though the wind was moderate the swell of the sea was greater than when we were exposed to the fury of a powerful Gale in the open ocean but it was a long steady swell of exceeding high waves with deep and awful Gulfs between them so that in the language of the Psalmist the ship was sometimes on the top of a mountain wave and at another in the deed [deep] abyss beneath yet she was not beaten about with so much violence as when the waters were driven by a furious wind[4] These straits are in some places 120 miles wide and in no part narrow enough for us to discern the land on either side when we are in the centre but there is a good many rocky Islands interspersed throughout the passage several of which we sailed close to without meeting with any accident About two days before our arrival in this channel we lost of a sudden the birds which had accompanied us in great numbers all the way from the Cape of Good Hope These were of different kinds but cheifly Cape Pigeons which are rather larger than a House Pigeon and marked all over with spots of Black and White and Albitrosses which are a very large bird some of them Grey some white & some brown [B]oth sorts with several others are flying day & night with only short intervals of rest on the water and they never go near the land except to lay their eggs and hatch their young The soldiers and sailors in our ship caught many albitrosses by throwing a strong hook baited with a peice of beef or pork into the sea and let it drag at the stern of the vessel They come around the ship most and are easiest caught in rough stormy weather. The most that was taken in one day was fifteen and the largest measured from the tip of one wing to the other eleven feet four Inches I have heard the sailors speak of catching some that measured 16 and 18 inches between the two extrimity of the wings but the one above mentioned is the largest I ever saw caught

When we got well into Bass Straits the heavy rolling sea we passed over at the entrance seemed to have subsided and we found ourselves in smooth water through which we made good way with a strong side wind and got clear of the channel by daylight the following morning Now for the first time the land of N. S. Wales appeared to our sight and the distance to Sydney was not greater than might have been performed in two days with a favourable wind but having calms and head winds it occupied us six days We came within sight of the lighthouse which stands at the entrance into the Harbour about Midday of the 25 of June and hoisted signals for a pilot who come on board about an hour after sunset in the evening at which we were very near the mouth of the Harbour A gentle breeze occasioned a ripple on the water whitch glittered beneath the beams of the full moon and so far the scenery was beautiful but the lofty rugged rocks at the entrance and sterile appearance of the land within the mouth of the Harbour was quite of a different character. The passage from the ocean is not half a mile wide and the rocks on both sides are exceeding high and being nearly perpendicular they looked by moonlight almost like regular built walls Just within these headlands the water expands and all the way to Sydney a distance of 7 miles it forms a number of inlets and harbours and extensive bays leaving projecting lands and Islands most of which are nothing but piles of rocks with a few stunted shrubs growing on them On one of these projecting lands that run a good way into the water Sydney is built which situation gives it a great advantage in the loading & unloading of Ships as the two sides and one end of the town fronts the water which for the most part is deep enough for ships to come close to the land. At about a quarter before nine oclock we arrived within a mile of the town and after firing a gun dropped anchor just completing our voage in just 18 weeks All was now conjecture and surmise as to our future destiny which state of suspense continued some time for we remained in the ship till Monday July 11th. on which day we landed & went to Hyde Park Barracks from whence we understood we were to be assigned to masters Some were called out within a few hours after we arrived there some on the following day and so on On the fifth morning it came to my turn The person who came for me took me to the Kings Wharf from whence I was to go in a boat up the river to Parramatta but as the [*wind*] was strong and unfavourable we could not sail till the evening [D]uring this days stay on the beach I felt more keenly than I had hitherto done the awkwardness of my situation Though I had left my home & native country several months still I had enjoyed my brother with 131 others of my countrymen who (although I knew but two of them before we entered the ship) were from parts not very remote from my home and what rendered it more pleasant they were for the most part men of honest principle but now how differently was I situated I was surrounded by persons I had been told possesed every vice without a single virtue and from what I saw and heard that day I thought they amply justified that report My things was put into the taproom of a hotel that was close by the wharf & I was to stay there myself till the boat started but I preferred the street for I had not been there long when an old drunken man began quarreling with a woman who I judged was a charwoman who was also drunk A little girl apparently about 9 or 10 years of age came to the assistance of her fair companion and laid the old man on with a stick a general squabble ensued between the three in which the old mans hat met with very rough usage and his head fared much the same for I perceived the blood flowing copiously down his face How long the affray might have continued I know not but the master of the hotel heard the quarrel and came and ordered the woman and the girl to their work and the man out of doors [T]he latter obeyed but seemingly with reluctance but not until he had poured out a volley of oaths & threats against his antagonists nor were the females any way sparing in returning the compliment This and the direful execrations that I heard in the streets in common discourse convinced me that I had not been misinformed when the character of the inhabitants was painted in dark colours But I felt myself awkward in another respect Myself and Robert took with us two sovereigns each which we were persuaded to give into the hands of the Doctor of the ship with a promise that it would be returned when we arrived at Sydney But instead of that the money was put into the savings Bank and we found we were not to have it till we became free or received tickets of leave [W]e had but one halfcrown between us out of which we purchased six pennyworth of Bread that in the barracks being so bad we could not eat it [T]his reduced our stock to two shillings and when I was called out we knew not how many days Robert might stay there so I took sixpence and left eighteenpence I had nothing to eat in the morning before we left the barracks nor was there anything for me where I stopped and as the day passed on I grew both hungry and thirsty and not having tasted beer since I left England I thought out of my sixpence I would afford myself one Glass but when I come to offer my money which I did before drinking the beer I found that the person were we changed the halfcrown had taken advantage of our ignorance of the coins in circulation and given us a small peice of Indian Silver that was not current but as it was silver a person that stood by told me he would take it for a plaything for his children and pay for the glass of beer if I liked and to this I agreed as the silver was of too trifling a value to go to a silversmiths with even if I knew where to find one.

Now picture to yourself my situation I who had scarced moved beyond the precints of the humble domicile which had been my abode from my boyish days and who knew nothing of society beyond the few rural villages around me with the exception of the last three years of my residence in England when I became acquainted with yourself and three or four others out of the village I whose knowledge of the world was little more than that of a hermit was now suddenly removed to the opposite side of the Globe & placed in another hemisphere 16000 miles from my native land friendless & pennyless and an hungred amid utter strangers of the vilest description and ignorant as to what my future destiny would be While I stood in the street near the door of the Tap musing over the change I experienced the first mate of the ship I came out in came along and recognising me accosted me asked to whom I was assigned and how I was going [H]e asked me moreover if I had had anything to eat to which I answered in the negative he then took me in and gave me some bread & cheese and beer Of the latter he would have given me a great deal more than was necessary if I would have accepted it but when I refused he gave me a shilling wished me good luck and departed. My wants were for that time supplied, soon after which the boatmen told me they were going to start The sun was now drawing near the horizon and as the wind had become more moderate and favourable we glided off up the river in pretty good stile the banks of which presented the same rocky barrenness of soil as the projecting rocks or Islands about the harbour only that in some places there grew large and lofty timber instead of low stunted shrubs When we got about half way up the river it became so dark that I saw nothing of the upper part at that time but in one place the boatmen deviated a little from the deep channel and run aground which occupied them some little time in getting right again Soon after this they drew the boat to the side of the river and went up into the wood to what they called the halfway house where they stayed an hour or more so that by the time we arrived at the place where they were to put me down namely my masters house on the bank of the river two miles out of Parramatta it was got late and they were all gone to bed so that I went on into Parramatta and stayed at one of the boatmans house the remainder of the night and the following morning he went with me to my masters who is a wealthy settler of the name of Macarthur[5] He told me that he intended sending me to a farm of his up the country but that I should stay there and work in the garden a week or two first The following day was Sunday but as I was an utter stranger there I chose to stay in the hut in the garden all day and not attempt to go from home On Saturday night a man came down from the farm I was to go with a dray loaded with hay and straw and hearing that I was just come from England he was soon at the hut on Sunday morning as almost everyone there seems glad to see a person on his first arrival and hear what news they can from their native country and in this instance it was consolatory to myself for though I had no previous knowledge of him yet he was born within two miles of my native home and had lived as carter at Mr Lewis of Barton Stacey and was acquainted with persons I knew so that we had a long chat together and I spent the greater part of the day with him which though it was a consolation I had not anticipated yet nevertheless led me to reflect that I had spent happier days at the place ton [to/on] which our conversation frequently turned In my new abode a fresh species of work devolved upon me which gave me no little uneasiness I had to wash my own shirt all the way out in [*the*] ship but now I had to cook my own victuals rather than do which in England I would have gone without one meal at any time but not many following I daresay Here I may as well describe to you what a hut is and how the people (free and bond) live in all the country parts of N. S. Wales At a distance round about the farm buildings is erected a number of huts which vary in length from 12 to 20 feet and in width they are 8 or 10 feet [T]hey are mostly built of Slabs split out of the trees in the forest and set upright allowing about 6 inches to go into the ground and 6 or 7 feet above it [T]he sides or rather edges of the Slabs are sometimes trimmed a little with an axe or adze and sometimes not and as they are frequently put up green and shrink afterwards it is as common as otherwise to see crevices 2 and 3 inches apart between the two slabs [A] post is put into the ground at each corner of the hut and poles laid on them and fastened down by wooden pins the tops of the slabs are nailed to these poles and then 6 or 8 rafters on a side are put up [S]ome large sheets of bark that is stripped from the trees an[d] tied to the rafters with strings of Green hide and thus the hut is completed with the exception of a fire place which is made of Slabs also and projects outwards so as not to interfere with the strait line of the hut inside. Sometimes the inside of the Slab place is plastered with clay 4 or 5 inches thick and two foot high but more frequently it remains bare till a cart load of ashes accumulate which form a bank all round for the protection of the Slabs from fire When a hut is built as above described the men are put into it varying in number from 2 to 6 and sometimes 8 [T]he furniture or rather utensils consists of an Iron pot and Frying pan for general use with an axe to cut wood and a quart tin to each Individual to boil tea in and sometimes a pint pannican to drink it out of A peice of coarse stuff which they call Ossenburgh is served out to each man who is a prisoner for a bed tick which he has to sew up himself and stuff with straw. If the men have other conveniences in the hut they must provide them themselves and in most instances Sunday is the only time they have for providing them If they do not choose to lay their bed on the ground which from the Innumerable quantity of fleas and ants and the like would be very uncomfortable to say nothing of the hazard of finding a snake coiled up in the blanket they must take an axe to the bush and cut some forked sticks and poles [T]he forked sticks are driven into the ground about three feet from the side of the hut and a pole laid into the forks while another pole is made fast to the slabs at an equal height and three or four short sticks laid across on which is placed a sheet of bark and the business of constructing a bedstead is over. But any one who disapproves of the above methods is quite at liberty to adopt any plan he please [A] sheet of bark or a few boards when they can be obtained placed on a rude frame serves for a table which is sometimes made fast to the side of the hut or fixed in the centre and sometimes it is portable They mostly contrive to make a stool or two which with a few blocks of wood forms seats for the whole of the occoupants This I assure you is a fair description of a hut in N. S. Wales for though some few may be a trifle better than what I have stated they are rare to be found and many are worse if that can be. And were a person altogether unacquainted with the country to stand at a little distance and from a farm and see as I have from 20 to 30 of these huts stuck up round it he could I think hardly be persuaded without ocular evidence that they were the abode of human beings who had their origin in a civilized country Many cowsheds and pigsties that I have seen in England for regularity and solidity of building and in exterior appearance are palaces compared with these huts Well into a hut of this description I was put in the garden at Parramatta in company with one other here I had to cook my meat and bake my bread. I witnessed the latter performance before I attempted it myself and though I knew that hunger would compel me to eat it I fancied at that time that I never should like the Bread In most huts they keep a sheet of bark on purpose to make the dough on and the following is the whole process of baking Put as much flour as you think proper on the bark shake a little salt amongst it, wet it up with water, well knead it and press it flat then scrape a place clean on the hearth about the size of your cake clap it down and cover it over with hot ashes and there let it remain from $\frac{3}{4}$ of an hour to an hour and a half according to the size of your cake then take it out and beat [*the*] ashes off with any thing you like a cows tail is frequently kept in the hut for that purpose This sort of bread I soon learned to make and I liked it very well after the first day or two I remained in the hut and worked in the garden at Parramatta between 10 and 11 weeks for the first fortnight there was only the person I found in it and myself after which we had three more companions and it was anything but a comfortable life The garden was about 4 acres but more than half of it was never dug with a spade only broke up as deep as it could be with large heavy hoes and then the potatoes and cabbage plants put into it This I thought was a slovenly way but I found by experience, in subsequent years that it matters little how it is done for the heat and drought of summer scorches up and frequently quite destroys that on which have been bestowed a great deal of labour as well as that which has been hurried over. The garden laid along by the side of a creek across which a dam was built about seven feet high for the purpose of keeping a supply of water for the garden as well as for the use of the house the river on which the boats came up from Sydney being only a narrow arm of the sea and consequently as salt as the ocean [T]here was no spring or stream of running water but the dam kept back the rain water, which drained from the hills into it, forming a pool about 400 yards long and from 4 to 6 feet deep and there being there as well as in every part of the country a thick strata of hard red clay underneath the top soil it holds water almost as well as an earthen vessel; but in that hot country during the long droughts a great deal if not all of the water thus dammed up is absorbed by the sun's rays; and when part remains, from its stagnant position, it is scarcely fit for use. The soil of the garden for a few yards from the waters edge is deep and black. Though loose and sandy and not capable of standing dry weather. At about 6 yards from the water it suddenly changed to a grey colour and was very shallow, being hard bad working land, and poor in quality, as was the whole of the land for a mile or more around my masters house, which house is about 2 miles out of the town and is called Vineyard Cottage. The second sunday I was there I went into Parramatta to the Church which stands on the south side of the Town And is a tolerable neat & Commodious building erected in the year 1800. A pretty large concourse of people seemed to assemble at this church on the Sunday in question and likewise on each subsequent Sunday during my stay at Vineyard Cottage. There is also in the town a Methodist Chapel where the service used to commence at 9 oclock or soon after and conclude soon enough for those who chose to go to church after. I sometimes went there in the morning and frequently in the evening.[6] It is rather small but a very neat building and was generally pretty full But if one quarter of those that attended both places were devout worshippers of god I know not where they kept themselves when away from Church or Chapel for I am sorry to say among the community at large it is a rare thing to find one who will not drink to excess quarrel fight make use of the most vile language that tongue can utter and overreach where he has it in his power Parramatta stands at the head of the salt water 16 miles from

Sydney and would I have no doubt enjoy a pretty good trade but for the shallowness of the river which prevents any but very small vessels from going up to town [T]he streets are formed out and run straight across each other except one which winds considerably and has a lofty wooden bridge over the river The town is stretched over a wide surface of land and there are many very good brick and stone houses but they are here one & yonder another and there are not above two or three good rows of buildings in the whole place The streets are wide & in most of them have raised footways on each side By the side of the footpath runs a fence of paling and the houses stand 12 or 14 feet farther back with open spaces in front But from what I could learn all the good buildings with the exception of the Church & hospital have been erected since about 1818: the best of those which are older have only one story and are weather boarded round the sides & have shingled roofs while not a few are built of slab & covered with bark, so that altogether the town has but a ragged appearance. A little way out of the town on the western side stands a Government House surrounded by a large domain and which domain is by the by as I was Informed inclosed by a Mahogany fence. This was the favourite residence of Sir Richard Bourke though the government House is much larger and stands up so as to command a good view of the Harbour I saw by the newspapers before I left that country that orders were sent out by the Home Government for the House & domain at Parramatta to be sold There is no river or stream of water near Parramatta but several deep creeks or gullies which bring the water from the hills when it rains unite in one at the head of the salt water where a strong stone dam is built to keep the fresh water back and from this reservoir the town is supplied by persons who draw it round in Casks There is barracks here for prisoners as well as at Sydney with barracks for the military, a court house & Jail which with the church & hospital is I beleive the whole of the public buildings in the town and this is all I have to say about Parramatta at present During my stay at Vineyard Cottage I went two or three Sundays in the afternoon for a walk with a shipmate as much as 6 or 7 miles out of Parramatta partly on flat land by the side of the river and partly over some high hills on the north Side from whose summits I had the first extensive view of the forest of new south wales or which is more commonly called Australia From the top of these hills we could very distinctly see the Blue Mountains of which I shall speak by & by they were not above 40 miles distant in a direct line but a person who was with me assured me that they could not be reached in less than 70 in a circuituos route from the perpendicular hills and deep ravines which lay between us & them though it appeared like a dead level or rather a gradual rise all the way But I found afterwards when I was up the country how deceiving the forest is in this respect If you get on an eminence where you can see 60 or 80 miles, hills 3 times as high as Bacon [Beacon] Hill between Newbury & Whitchurch, with valleys 2000 feet deep between them are not perceivable but the farthest land the eye can distinguish plainly looks like a range of lofty mountains & all between appears to be an extensive plain and a dismal black scenery it is. So it was on the high hills above mentioned we could see mountains at an immense distance all around us and the intervening space seemed to be one vast hollow or circular plain destitute of variety or beauty. The eminence of which I am speaking is a range of Hills which if viewed at a little distance appears to be but one but when you come on them you find them divided by narrow abrupt valleys 200 & 300 feet deep They are called Pennant Hills most of them are cleared of timber and there are a number of small farms on and about them as there is also on a tract of lower land near them called The Field of Mars. From these settlements we crossed over some flattish land and come to the river, not far from where the boat run aground when I was coming up from Sydney. There is a point of land where there is a Wharf and about which live several small settlers besides one wealthy one of old standing in the colony a Major Lockyer[7] The place is called Kissing Point and I will tell you why it is so called to shew from what simple occurences places derive their names After governor Philip (who established the Colony) and the officers that went out with him had made them tents and such like where now stands Sydney, they sailed up the river landing at several different Places & among the rest at the point above alluded to and while they were strowling about among the trees some one saw the governor kiss his lady and this point of land has ever been distinguished from others by the appelation of Kissing, and since Steam navigation has been established on the river you will see in the papers that they stop there to discharge & take in passengers that the fare is so much from Parramatta and so much from Kissing Point The river has a great number of branches or arms all the way up many of which go a good way back into the forest and so much resemble the principal channel that strangers have great difficulty in finding their way from Sydney to Parramatta. I had 3 or 4 Sundays walk along the margin of the river & about the settlements in the neighbourhood & having heard so much about the fertility of N. S. W. I was struck at beholding the sterility which presented itself on all sides the only exceptions I saw being a few spots on the Penant Hills and at the Field of Mars. And when I spoke of this to the Gardeners at my masters he told me that the land about Parramatta & Sydney was some of the worst in the country that if I could see the fields of beautiful corn & grass in the direction of the Cowpastures I should say no more about the barreness of the country or think any more of England.

I felt an inward consciousness that the latter part of this assertion would never be verified and how far the former talk was deserving of Credit you will be able to judge after I have given you a sketch of my five years and a half residence in that District While I was at Parramatta I received a Letter from Robert which cost me 4d out of the shilling which the first mate of Ship gave me. Robert was still in the barracks at Sydney but expecting to go every day to one Major Sullivan of Williamse's

River.[8] As I was expecting every week that I should go up the country I wrote a letter for home leaving only space to mention the day of my departure if I should have the opportunity. On the 26th. of Sep$^{r.}$ I received information that I was to go by the dray the driver of which was the man who came to see me the first Sunday I was in the garden. On the following day we started taking in the dray an old meat safe a few old chairs & a mattrass and some blankets with one of the menservants from the house. The carter had to take up 30 bushels of lime in Parramatta & while he was at that I went to the Post Office with my letter for England the Postage for which I found to be 8d just the money I had left so that I started off up the country unburdened with money It was 3 oclock in the afternoon before we left the town and as the oxen were poor & weak for want of grass and the distance we had to go being 30 miles we did not expect to reach home that night. About 2 miles out of the town we stopped at a hut by the side of the Road where we got some water (oftentimes a scarce article on the roads in N. S. Wales) and made some tea after drinking which & eating a peice of damper (cake Baked on the hearth) and salt beef we set out on our journey in earnest along a way called Dogtrap Road. The timber on both sides of this road have been cut down some years ago & young trees sprung up again either from the roots or seeds of the old ones much thicker than the original forest and as these saplings were from 20 to 30 feet high & occupied a space of 30 yards on each side of the road they precluded all view of the country around. At about 6 miles from Parramatta this road unites with the Sydney turnpike and proceeds to Liverpool, Campbell Town, Bong Bong, Goulbourn, Yass, & the whole southern territory of the Colony When we got into this road the sides were more open on which stood a few huts & two or three Public Houses the latter being weatherboarded round the sides & covered with shingles instead of bark but none of them have any more than one floor. We reached Liverpool (9 miles from Parramatta) just before sunset and as our carter had a place or two to call at it was quite dusk when we left it. There is a hospital two story high built of red bricks with a spacious yard around it enclosed by a brick wall It appears to be very clean, neat, and airy place and has that name from persons who have been in it There is also a large brick church, a lunatic asylum, a court house and Jail. Besides this there are 2 good inns 3 or 4 shops and about a dozen neat private dwelling houses the remainder of the town is comprized of weather boarded houses of one story and a parcel of huts. But like Parramatta some regularity seems to have been observed in planning out the town for most of the streets run straight across each other and have fences at the side but the houses are so thinly scattered over a large space of land that it will be many years before the vacancies are filled up. A want of good water is a great inconvenience to the inhabitants & the land for miles around is of the most barren description being a sandy surface intermixed with gravel and looks of a pale rusty colour. And there was not a bit more grass to hide the naked surface of the land than there is blades of wheat at this time (Feby 5) to cover the feilds of England after a month of hard frost with sharp cutting winds As soon as we got out of Liverpool it became quite dark so that for the next 7 miles I saw nothing of the road but at the 7 miles end or thereabout we met with an accident which detained us till the following morning We had just passed the last Public House that we should see (so our carter told us) & were ascending a long hill part of which had been cut along the side leaving a high bank to the right hand & a deep ravine on the left where was some rails as a safeguard to vehicles going along the road. The bullocks were got tired & instead of ascending the hill when they come to the pinch they run backwards driving the dray against the rails which seemed to be put there more for show than strength for they suddenly gave way but luckily the jerk shook the iron pin out which held the bullocks to the pole of the dray which saved them but the dray soon disappeared & as the night was very dark & everything strange to me I could form no conjecture how far it was gone only I could hear some of the contents rattle a good way down the side of the Hill There was a man laying on the dray at the time & we were apprehensive that he must either be killed or seriously injured & our fears seemed for a time to be confirmed as we called repeatedly without receiving any answer but after a minute or so he crawled out from under the lime and bedding & hollowed to us to say that he was not hurt Our driver then unyoked his bullocks & put them into a paddock on the opposite side of the road after which we [*climbed*] down to examine the dray & we found it had not gone so far as I expected the declivity not being very rapid close to the road However though it started upright we found it turned up on one side & all of its contents emptied out in confusion & some of the lime probably gone to the bottom of the valley As it was very dark all that we could do was to rear the dray on its legs & pull the blankets &c out from under the lime & make us a bed under the dray where we laid till daylight when we arose to examine the wreck & found to our utter astonishment & delight that the dray remained sound in every part & no injury worth naming was done to any of the load with the exception of the lime a good part of which was wasted among the dirt dead leaves & rotten wood that covered the surface of the ground We went back to the public house we passed the night before where we borrowed a shovel an iron pot & some water & returned to our camp where we made a fire to boil our tea in the iron pot After breakfast we scraped up what lime we could & reloaded our dray then yoked the bullocks & made a fresh start but we had to go a considerable way back before we could get into the road again. We returned the shovel & pot & after regaining the road proceeded gently onward over a dreary lonesome tract of country a distance of 13 or 14 miles to our destination, seeing but two farms all the way & meeting with nothing worth relating only that the land was hilly & appeared quite as barren as any about Parramatta. The farm at which we arrived & which was to be my abode is called Westwood & stands on the north bank of the Nepean River My master had a little cottage built at the farm for his accomodation when he chose to come up & stay a few days This cottage was not quite finished when I got there & the carpenter plasterer &c with their assistants were living in huts round about the farm some of them were married & some not in all there was 5 women on the farm 3 of whom was very soon drunk from a keg of rum we took up in the dray And here I may as well inform you that the settlers are allowed to retail spirits on their farm in exchange for labour & knowing how much the people of that country are addicted to rum drinking they seldom fail to have a supply for that purpose when they have free men working for them & 5/s a bottle is the common retail price in that neighbourhood at which rate a gallon fetches about 28/s & costs in Sydney from 10 to 12 shillings At this rate of dealing with rations proportionably dear I have known many persons to be in debt to their masters after doing as much work as come to 60 or 70 pounds But I shall tell you more of this hereafter The rum we took up was drank pretty freely by men & women & it was not long before one of the latter fell into the fire but without being burnt any to signify after this she attempted to walk to her hut a distance of about a ¼ of a mile but when she had accomplished about 50 yds. she fell down like a stone & there she lay till taken up & carried home The 2nd. of the drunken women must needs go to get a young cow in the milking bails where she pulled at the rope & swore as bad as any sailor & was sometimes on her feet & sometimes not so But after pulling as long as she liked she contrived to get home without being carried The 3rd.

woman got drunk at home so that she only had to go to bed when she could maintain her equilibrium no longer. The other two women as far as I saw remained sober but the drinking blackguardism and quarreling that I saw & heard that afternoon convinced me that the people up the country were of the same stamp as those in Sydney & Parramatta.

There was a small building called a kitchen detached from the cottage at Westwood in which lived a free man & his wife & I was there to have my victuals & to sleep in the cottage at night but my rations were weighed out to me just the same as the other prisoners [T]his ration consists of 7 lbs. of beef 1 peck of wheat 1 lb. of sugar 2 ozs. tea & 2 oz. tobacco the three last named articles are not given by order of the government but left to the discretion of the master & are called indulgences[9] The tobacco I did not receive as I never used any & they will not give it to a person who do not use it There was a steel mill on the farm & we had to grind the wheat ourselves after we had done work & sift & bake it in the manner I have told you There was a garden at Westwood measuring an acre & I was put to work among it & work enough I had for the only marks of former tillage was about 100 cabbage stumps in one bed & a few potatoe greens in another that had sprung from some small ones left in the ground The whole garden was as hard as a road covered with old dead weeds & grass & as the spring was far advanced I could do little good in it However I broke up part of it & put in some cabbage plants & some pumpkins & melon seeds But I was soon taken from the garden & put to every kind of odd jobs on the farm The land was sadly over run with couch grass & sometimes I have been for weeks raking up that behind the harrow & burning it Sometimes I was mowing & reaping & helping to get in the hay & wheat also hoeing between the rows of Indian Corn hilling it & in the season gathering it When wheat was to be winnowed I must always make one & to truss the hay & load the dray for Parramatta was sure to be my job with so many others that the garden was but badly attended to However the pumpkin & melon seeds I planted came up & I contrived to keep them alive by carrying some water to them when I could find time till the 11th. Jany. when we had a fine rain & I think I never saw anything thrive so fast as they did after that rain The vines soon spread over the bed I planted them in though a large one & across the paths which were 6 feet wide & fruit that was of the size of my thumb in 4 days was as large as my head & some of the pumpkins when they had attained their full size was as large as a 4 Gallon water bucket & proportionally long & the water melons though somewhat smaller yet grew to a very great size The paddocks at that time in some parts was actually white with mushrooms & I think I may say without exaggeration that if carefully gathered enough might have gathered in one morning to fill the bed of a waggon without going off our farm The grass also sprung up very rapidly & by the middle of April it was over a persons knees where 3 months before the surface of the ground was as bare as a turnpike road Here I must inform you that Jany. Feb^y. & March in N. S. Wales answers to July August & Sep[r.] in England only from that country's greater proximity to the Equator the heat far exceeds what is common during these months here: & as there was plenty of rain fell during the three first named months on the year in question it occasioned vegetation to proceed with that rapidity which I have described But I had soon to learn that such fertile seasons were of short continuance for by the latter end of April the face of the country assumed another colour & the grass which had grown so rapidly seemed about to decay with equal speed Soon after may commenced the nights were a little frosty with brisk drying winds by day which in a very short time deprived the autumnal grass of all its sap & rendered it lighter than feathers This grass never grows till after the longest days & is of a peculiar kind with a weak stem & flat spreading top growing according to the quantity of moisture & richness of the soil from 6 inches in height to 2 feet but in the latter case it always falls down the tops turning up again the stem being too weak to support it in an erect position It is called curren grass but I think from its speedy growth & decay a more suitable appelation would be mushroom grass it is indigenous to the country & makes tolerable good hay if cut in time but during my 6 years residence in that country I never knew it to grow in sufficient quantities to be worth cutting with the exception of the time above alluded to I have examined it minutely & I am inclined to believe that it is an annual grass & springs from the seed as the root dies with the stem in fact I have seen it grow & die in the garden just the same as annual weeds &

sometimes its period of existance is not more than 6 weeks. The first autumn that I was in the country when there was such abundance of it, it was all completely dead by the Middle of May & soon after when the winds blew strong it was broken off close to the ground & swept across the country in great rolls till it found something to stop it: so that large banks of it was frequently seen laying against the fences & of all substances I ever handled I think that was the lightest You might take up a large Armful & scarcely perceive that you held weight in your hands. By the 1st. of June of the year in question the whole of this grass was blown away & the blades of all the other sorts dead so that the gay green carpet that was spread over the hills & valleys about 3 months before was changed into a rusty garb to which the lands of England in the depth of winter bears no comparison but I know that after I have written as good a description of the country as my weak abilities will admit of & you have formed conjectures from that you will still be far from possessing a genuine knowledge of that distant part of the globe We are to[o] apt to ground our conceptions upon things & sceneries with which we are familiar to form correct ideas from the best descriptions of those of which we have no ocular testimony at least so it is with myself [F]or instance I have known dry summers in England & making allowances for N S Wales being a hotter country I tried to form in my imagination what it would be there but had I not seen it I should have been greatly astray in my conjectures May June & July are the winter months there & the weather is tolerably pleasant sometimes there are white frosts by night but they are very slight & disappear soon after the sun is up in the morning & the middle of the day is very warm The shortest day (June 21st.) is 9 hours & 46 minutes Augst. Sepr. Octr. are spring months & I doubt not but the average heat of the 2 latter in general would be greater if taken than that of any 2 months of the year in England Novr. Decr. Jany. are summer months & very great heat prevails throughout that period & in general but little rain falls Feby. March and April are Autumnal months the 2 first of which are extremely hot & the latter as warm as our Sepr. I have taken the liberty of dividing the year as above myself others might prefer placing them exactly the reverse of the seasons here & call Decr. Jany. Feby. the summer months & so on. So utterly diverse from England is the country in its appearance & physical productions that could you without previous knowledge be removed suddenly from this country & placed in that beyond the cultivated districts you might almost think you had taken a trip to some other planet for the sun & moon though they rise in the east go to the left and shine from the north while most of the stars in the northern hemisphere are there excluded from view & a great number towards the South Pole appear that are not visible here while the earth is clothed with timber not one tree of which you could call by name & the grass & herbage such as it is differs in like manner from that of England. The birds & beast are also different from ours with very few exceptions one of which is the black crow a bird that much resembles those of this country in size note & plumage & which it seems are to be found in every country throughout the world. But there is one singular circumstance connected with those of N S Wales & that is though they are to be seen in considerable numbers at all seasons of the year yet no person (black or white) could ever find one of their nests I have heard that considerable rewards have been offered for a nest of young ones but I will not be answerable for the truth of that There are quails too which are not unlike ours but they are not plentiful The next is the swallow which are shorter & smaller than ours & do not sing but wherever may have been the place of their nidification before there was any buildings in the country they now seek the habitations of men & mostly make their nests between the rafters inside of the sheds There are wild pigeons also about as large as a house pigeon & sometimes they are to be seen in considerable numbers & sometimes you will scarce see a dozen in a year These with the exception of now and then a mute lark & two sorts of hawks one about the size of our sparrow hawks & the other somewhat larger are the only birds that I remember to have seen which resemble the birds of England The dissimilarity among the beasts is still greater, the wild dog being the only one I know that is anything like the beasts of England. So that was [*you*] in the bush & did not chance to see any of the birds mentioned or a dog you would scarcely be certain that you was on our planet You would find no Victoria Omnibusses nor see anything of a Railroad but from the highest hill you could ascend you would have to view a dense & gloomy forest on all sides as far as the eye can reach Even in what is called the thickly settled districts I have sought the highest eminences from whence the cleared portions of land appeared like dots or specks in the immeasureable woods around them while many of 100 or 200 acres that lay in a low situation could not be seen at all [S]ome of the settlers have from 20 000 to 30 000 acres in one spot & often not more than 300 or 400 acres cleared & sometimes less & as each one selects the best land for cultivation it may happen that the cleared portions are at the opposite sides of the estates leaving 6 or 7 miles of bush between & it seldom happens that there is less than a mile of bush between the cleared lands of two neighbouring estates Here I may just mention that all land in the state of nature is indiscriminately termed the bush though for miles together there is nothing but timber which in general is large & lofty but not so thick but a cart may be driven between the trees with ease [T]o the N.E. of Westwood we had to go through 6 miles of bush to reach the nearest farm, on the N side was 2 miles on the NW 5 miles on the W & WNW 2 miles each but though the farm buildings of one of those was two miles from us the cleared lands was seperated only by about 600 yards of bush [T]o the S.W. the neighbouring farm was ? miles off & bush good part of the way to the S & SE there was several little settlers within 3 miles who rented from 30 to 50 acres each of a person who had a considerable tract of land in that direction to the E it was about 4 miles through the bush to the nearest farm After passing 2 farms to the W of Westwood distant 2 miles you then entered the bush in earnest there being no settlements till you get to Bathhurst on the Western side of the Blue Mountains a distance I should think of more [*than*] 100 miles When I first went to Westwood ours was the westernmost farm in that tract of country but during my stay there others were formed & 600 or 700 acres of land was divested of its natural burden & I saw large fields of corn growing before I left it on the very spot where the first year I was there I witnessed the feats of the blacks called a corroberee performed by night in the thick & gloomy forest Seasons for sowing & planting & harvesting The best time for sowing wheat is in April & May as that which is sown in June is often in a green state when the hot winds begin to blow in Nov$^{r.}$ & then it is almost sure to be spoiled or so much injured as to be worth but little But there is no certainty when these hot winds will commence I have known them to blow in April & May [*Wheat*] will mostly be ripe by the middle of Nov$^{r.}$ but as there is a little difference in the seasons & as some sorts of wheat do not ripen so soon as others by a fortnight I may say the time of wheat harvest lies between the middle of Nov$^{r.}$ & the end of Dec$^{r.}$ although one harvest we did not commence reaping till the 28th. Dec$^{r.}$ & finished on the 26th. Jan$^{y.}$ But this was an unusual occurence & I heard it remarked by persons who had been 20 years in the country that they never knew it so late before It was occasioned by the drought which was long & severe no rain falling worth mentioning from the middle of Sep$^{r.}$ 1834 to March 31st. 1836 Wheat sown in April and May did not vegetate till the

Sep[r.] following when there was a few partial showers which brought it above ground but much of it only come up to die & some little shot up 6 or 8 inches high and formed a small ear but half that fell down flat on the ground & the harvest such as it was, was rather gathered than reaped as many persons did not use a hook but pulled up & scraped together what they could. We had $2\frac{1}{2}$ bushels to the acre on our farm & a little settler that I knew 3 miles from us had 32 small sheaves off 4 acres of land while on Shancamore Estate[10] 2 miles from us they had 100 bushels of threshed wheat (I will not say clean wheat) from 150 acres of land & there were thousands of acres in many parts of the country where they never attempted to gather any Some turned their cattle & pigs into the fields while others drawed a bush harrow over the ground to brush cut [out] and scatter what little seed was matured enough to grow & then ploughed it in trusting to it for their next years crop Oats are mostly sown as soon as the wheat is finished as the winters are never severe enough to injure them & they do much better than if sown in the spring but the dry hot weather is most sure to set in & spoil them They are a very uncertain crop & few settlers in the part of the country where I was attempt to save more for seed than what they think will be sufficient for themselves & many not even that preferring purchasing those in Sydney that are brought up from Van Diemens Land The best of seed in about 3 years becomes quite wild & little better than the seed of the Kangaroo grass which grow in the bush Nearly their whole use is to make hay for which they are cut as soon as the ear is well formed It makes very good hay when well managed & horses fed on it do well Lucerne is the next best grass for making hay & the seed should be sown about the same time as wheat & oats. I saw a few feilds of it that did very well Clover & rye grass such as is common in England should also be sown about the same time (as it is no use to sow any small seeds in the spring) and I have heard persons say that they have seen good crops of hay made of such grasses but for my own part during my 6 years residence there I never knew any of the seed of such to be sown or saw any of it growing Winter barley is likewise sown in the Autumn in small quantities to cut up green for horses or milch cattle but it is no use for malting & pig fattening is out of the question Barley such as is common in England I was told was grown in the cooler parts to the south & I saw about 6 bushels grow on our farm one year which was the whole I saw while in the country It is too tender to stand the white frosts of the winter & if sown in the spring it is destroyed by the drought and heat The best season for sowing turnips is Feb[y.] March & the beginning of April Of these months March is the best time for all sorts but as the Swedish turnips requires a longer time to come to maturity it is best to sow them in Feb[y.] if there should chance to be any rain You might as well throw seed in the fire as attempt to grow turnips in the spring They might grow & come out in rough leaf & in general that would be the extent of their growth & should there be moisture enough to keep a few of them alive they would all run to seed & not one of them would form a head. I have seen some very good turnips by the latter end of May when they have been sown in March but as the winters are mild they soon start up to seed & are not good above 5 or 6 weeks & I think I might say there is not above 1 settler out of 6 or 7 that attempts to grow any Like all other Crops thay are very uncertain as the drought often prevail in the Autumn as well as at other seasons of the year Maize or Indian Corn is planted in October & is seldom ripe till May & sometimes the beginning of June following. It is planted in rows of 5 feet apart by men who carry it in small bags tied around their waists & a hoe in their hands with which they scrape away the earth about 2 inches deep & then drop the Grains & pull the mould over them & repeat the same at every 4 or 5 feet The Plough is drawn along making slight scratches 5 feet apart for a guide to the planters & now & then a settler who is more particular than the Majority of them will have the plough drawn across the first lines cutting the whole field into squares and then plant 5 grains in every corner thus  & when the corn is high & strong enough men go through it & with hoes draw up a large bank of earth round every bunch of corn which stand 5 feet asunder each way [T]he best crop I saw was on Mr. Mannings farm at Vermont about 2 miles from us & that averaged at 20 bushels to the acre & some of it measured 16 feet in height[11] I have known it to average at almost every number of bushels under 20 down as low as 2 according to the Quality of the Land & the favourableness or otherwise of the seasons & I have seen numbers of Acres completely destroyed by the drought Potatoes are planted in July & August for the summer crop but I never saw one of those Crops that would pay for the digging up. They are as good as ever they will be by Christmas & vary in size from a horse bean to a crows egg It sometimes happens that a Thunder shower comes when they are formed in which case they do not grow larger but send out fresh germs & form another potatoe & I have dug them up when there was 5 or 6 all on a string a few inches apart about as large as marbles & shrivelled with the heat & drought like baked apples [T]hey are planted with better success sometimes in Janry. & Febry. & as they come in by the begginning of May they keep good nearly 3 months Out of the 6 years I was there we had 2 very fair Crops at that season & I believe might have had a 3rd. but for want of seed to plant. Pumpkins Melons & Cucumbers must be planted in Sepr. & Octr. but they seldom flourish much till Jany. unless in situations where they can be well watered [T]he best season for planting peas is in April as they grow very well in the winter & are fit to gather in Septr. Beans should be planted at the same time but they are an uncertain crop they blossom well but the greater part of it falls of without leaving any pods as a remedy for which I have lopped them at almost every stage of their growth but it made no difference I never saw but about half a crop Dwarf Kidney beans bear well oftentimes when planted in Jany. & Feby. but the spring Crop is seldom succesful & the scarlet runners will not do at any season I have planted them myself & known others to plant them & they blossom extremely well but it all falls of I had 15 given me one year which I planted & took all the care I could of them & all got was 4 these I attended to with greater care the next year & formed a bank all round them making [a] basin that would contain 4 or 5 buckets of water. This ditch I used to fill & when it soaked away lay some light dung on the earth to prevent the sun drying it up but after all my trouble I had not a single Bean & so I lost my stock You cannot rise plants in the Autumn to produce cabbage in the spring as we do in England for any plant so reared will be sure to run to seed & those which grow early in the spring seldom come to cabbage till after the height of summer Jan[y.] is about the best season for putting out plants though Feb[y.] & March do very well if the seasons are kind 2 years out of the 6 I was there we had abundance of good cabbage during the winter, the other 4 years it failed Radishes lettuce mustard cress & such like may be grown in the Autumn & winter sometimes but the summers are too hot and dry for all kinds of vegetables in general & at best they are greatly inferior to those of England Persons who have been in the habit of seeing a crop of vegetables succeed the planting so regularly here in England when they arrive at N S Wales & see the gardens so bare are mostly inclined to think that the fault is attributable to those who manage them & think they could do better themselves I was not quite free from thoughts of that kind myself for a time but experience soon taught me better yet I very well know that there is in many instances some of the roughest management in both Agriculture & Horticulture that I ever saw In the winter of 1834 we had a fresh overseer took charge of the farm who was then just come out from England & he wondered that we had no potatoes I told him that the summers were so dry & hot we could not get any to grow. He replied It is only because people here dont know how to manage them I'll make them grow you'll see that we'll have plenty of potatoes next winter This I knew would be a vain boast unless the season proved different from what they are in general Well the next winter come & we had no potatoes nor indeed a vegetable of any description for that was part of a 17 months drought Onions are a very uncertain crop but the only chance of getting them is to sow them in the Autumn soon enough for them to get pretty strong before winter & they will head tolerable well in the spring if there is a little moisture but it is difficult to save any onion seed it sometimes shows very well for a time but always or nearly so goes off with the blight or heat. Whether it arises from the heat & drought or the nature of the soil I cannot say but there is a great proneness in almost every vegetable to degenerate & run wild even when the greatest care is taken in saving the seeds I have had beans of the windsor & longpod kinds just as they came from England & as fine as I ever saw & the 3rd. crop what few there was was little better than horsebeans & the same of most other kinds of vegetables

Fruits

THE COUNTRY IN its original state produces no fruit will afford sustenance to man & those introduced from England with the exception of the peach do not flourish so well as they do here The only native fruits I saw was 2 sorts of black currants & a pear the latter grows on the tops of mountains & among rocks by the side of Creeks They are about as large as a middling sized pear of a gray colour & when at a little distance from them you would think you were going to have a fine feast but a close inspection finds them to be a substance as hard as wood defying anything less powerful than an axe to split them They are a perfect model of the English pears but as most things there are the reverse of what they are here in some way or another & so are these for the large ? grows on the branch. When kept a time they split of their own accord, & in the centre of which is a small kernel about the size of an Almond. One sorts of currants grows on a short scrub on the Mountains where they are gathered by the blacks who bring them round to the settlements & get a little tea sugar or tobacco for them. They are the most powerful acid I ever tasted for if you put a pound of sugar to a pint of them so as to make them a complete syrup still they will set your teeth on edge & you will find the effects of them in your teeth & gums for a day or two if you eat many of them The other sort grows on an annual plant that springs up in the cultivated lands & stands about a foot high with little spreading branches The fruit is as large as peas & sweetish but so sickening that I never could eat more than 10 or 12 at once Of the fruits that are introduced the peach does by far the best & the tree grows as if it were indigenous to the soil producing fruits in such quantities some years that bushels of them are given to the pigs Apple & Pear trees grow tolerable well in some parts & bear a few very large fruit but they & also the peaches are destitute of that fine flavour which pertain to the English fruits Apples & Pears in general are very scarce & middling sized ones will often sell in Sydney for threepence each & none will keep beyond a few weeks Plums & Cherries are still more scarce, of the former I did not see a ripe one during my abode in that country [I] have known them to grow to the size of small birds eggs & then all drop off & the trees will frequently blossom again in the Autumn as profusely as they do in the spring (which is not inferior to what we see them here) but no fruit follow at that season. I saw a few ripe cherries at different times in all perhaps about 2 pounds Gooseberries Currants & Raspberries do very bad there of the two latter I did not see one & of the former only 6 green ones about the size of peas all the six summers I was there Strawberries sometimes do very well we had a pretty good crop 3 seasons the others it was a failure with them Oranges do very well in the warm districts but they will not flourish on the elevated lands to the west & south I have seen very good crops of them in and about Parramatta & also in the Neighbourhood where I spent my time in one garden but they are not much cultivated being a tree that will not come into good bearing under 12 or 14 years & the people of that country cannot endure waiting long for anything They blossom all the year round and while the ripe fruit is hanging on the tree you will see green ones of various sizes also Lemons Citrons & Almonds are also cultivated but on rather a small sclele [scale] Loquets thrive well & bear great crops some years if taken care of. I beleive other fruits from tropical regions have been introduced but their culture is very limited & they never come under my observation Grapes do pretty well in some situations & a few of the old settlers have made several hogsheads of wine from them but it is not till within the last 4 years that the general attention seemed to be awakened thereafter almost every settler of any note has since that period been having a portion of ground trenched for a Vineyard & many of them have gone the length of laying some scheme to get a number of German Emigrants out there to manage them. But it was the opinion of Mr. Shepherd one of the best horticulturalists that the colony had that the formation of Gardens Orchards & Vineyards is next to useless unless some plan be adopted to irrigate them & here the grand obstacle is a want of water.[12] You might travel 40 or 50 miles perhaps without seeing a stream & if there are ponds they lay in the beds of deep creeks where the aid of machinery would be requisite to bring it up over the land to say nothing of the chance of their becoming dry just at the time their service would be most required. In most cases therefore it would be necessary in the first instance to raise an artificial supply of water & this certainly might be done by building dams across the creeks either of timber or stone to keep the water back in time of rain But for my part I would prefer building the dam across a valley where there was no creek so that the bottom of the water might be on the surface of the land Many places may be found where the valleys are broad & deep with a gradual descent & then suddenly become narrow with steep sides this would be a convenient place to make the dam 12 or 14 feet high with an arch a large cock or some other contrivance at the bottom to let the water through or stop it back as needful The garden or orchard must of course be below & ditches might be cut so as to let the water run to any part where it was wanted. The soil in every part of the colony lays on a bed of hard red clay through which the water cannot penetrate so that it holds water like an earthen vessel. If therefore the proprietor of a garden or orchard was to look out for a long valley which received the drainage from a range of hills he might by building dams sufficiently high & strong secure water enough for 12 or 15 months This might be done throughout the colony for gardens Orchards or Vineyards but I see no practicable means by which irrigation could be carried to an extent sufficient to benefit Corn crops for if engines were had recourse to [*to*] force water from the deep beds of rivers to the surface of the land still from the paucity of rivers & their diminutive description it could be done only on a small scale even then. The olive tree has been introduced into the country but have not received much attention being cultivated only in a very limited manner by a few of the wealthiest settlers I saw a few healthy trees in my masters's garden at Parramatta.

Geographical position face of the country rivers &c

N SOUTH WALES approaches to within 10 degrees of the Equator & exclusive of Van Diemens Land extend I think to the 40th. parallel of Southern latitude I forget how many degrees of longtitude it embraces but some persons affirm that it is larger than Europe while others say it is not so large viz nearly one fourth Swan River commonly called Western Australia is part of the same land & distant from Sydney 1800 miles Van Dieman's Land lay to the South being an Island about as large as England & seperated from the main Land by Bass Straits about 120 miles wide in some places The nearest seaport in this Island to Sydney is Launceston: which is 700 miles but the principal place Hobart Town is 1100 miles The soil & climate of Van Diemens Land it is said to be much more genial to the growth of wheat than N. S. Wales & there is a pretty good trade carried on between the two places Sydney stands at the very eastern extremity of what is now called the 5th. division of the Globe A range of lofty & abrupt hills called the Blue Mountains from 40 to 60 miles inland runs across the country nearly in a North & South direction from Sea to Sea forming one unbroken chain & dividing so much of the eastern territory from the main bulk of the land to the west. The part laying to the east of these mountains is what was at first called N. S. Wales that to the west New Holland while the whole territory united was called Australasia—or Southern Asia: but of late years it is called Australia & denominated Eastern Southern & Western Australia Botany Bay a name so well known in England & to which such a stigma is attached is a large & beautiful Sheet of water about 6 miles from Sydney overland and ten round the coast Governor Philip who was entrusted by the government of England with the formation of the Colony arrived in this bay in Jan[y.] 1788 where the settlement was to have commenced But the bay being large &

the land around it quite low no shelter is afforded to Shipping & in some other respects I believe he considered it defective & sailed on in quest of a more elgible place which he found in Port Jackson where he landed & commenced the task of planting a Colony on the 26th. of Jany. 1788 with 778 convicts of which 220 were women. About three miles from Westwood (the place where I lived) & 40 from Sydney is a hill which still bears his name & is likely to do so for ages to come. This hill formed the limits of his inland tour & pretty well too when we consider the density of the forest in those early times & the paucity of European inhabitants. On the top of this hill he had all the timber cut down & was preparing to build a telegraph Whether in this work he intended to prepare for generations to come or whether he meant it for his own time & had proceeded thus far before it come into his head that there was no inhabitants in the interior to convey news too I never heard & perhaps he never told any one but at any rate the scheme was abandoned & the place to this day is called Philip's Folly A round emininence towring somewhat above the rest on the Razor Back range & distant from Philip's Folly about 10 miles is honoured with the appelation of Mount Hunter as being the boundary of the travelling excursions of that governor who was successor to Governor Philip As the inhabitants increased private individuals in small parties explored the whole of the country up to the foot of the Blue Mountains, whose lofty & abrupt precipices seemed to defy an ascent & say to the adventurers "Hither may you come but no further". They were traced throughout their whole length but no passage or chasm appeared the same bold front presenting itself in every direction shutting out all intercourse with the western territory except by the sea. The rivers which rise on the eastern side of these Mountains are in general but insignificant streams having a short run to the sea but a day or two's rain will swell them to torrents by means of water from the mountains & ranges of hills Necessity at last accomplished what had been a long time considered impracticable The year 1817 was remarkably dry & hot & the cattle which had become pretty numerous were fast diminishing from the severity of the drought which set some of the most enterprizing Settlers to work to find if possible a way over the Blue Mountains Three of them at last succeeded after encountering many difficulties & hardships When the first struggle of ascending this bold natural barrier were completed they had about 50 miles of Barren Summit to pass over before they come in view of the plains & undulated lands to the west But they persevered until they descended & examined these Lands & finally placed their cattle upon them. The success of these colonists stimulated many others to like exertions & in a year or two a temporary road was formed over these rugged mountains & a settlement commenced to which the name of Bathurst was given in honour of Earl Bathurst who was at that time secretary for the colonies In a few years the new settlers had wheat and meat enough for their consumption but the difficulty of getting all other supplies from Sydney was incalcubable as all drays were obliged to be unloaded on reaching the foot of the mountains & the goods dragged up on sledges or carried on the backs of oxen

& this task had to be performed several times before gaining the top as the mountains rises by stairs as it were & I have heard persons affirm that to get up some of them they have had to take the wheels off their drays & drag them up one at a time & the dray & goods seperately Some alternative to escape this laborious task was eagerly sought for as the difficulty of descending was almost as great as that of ascending They used to cut down a large tree & chain it to the axletree so as to drag behind the dray & with both wheels locked slide down in the best way they could but accidents as you may well suppose were not unfrequent. It occured to the minds of some persons that a navigable river might be found on the Western side of the blue Mountains emptying itself in the ocean somewhere along the southern part of the country by which means their produce could be conveyed to market & supplies brought back, without encountering a journey over that terrific range A small river that run by the settlement that was formed & it was determined to trace it in its downward course which task was entrusted to a Mr. Oxley the then Colonial surveyor who with a party & provisions for the journey penetrated the forest & traced the river (called the Macquarie) till they found it enter an impassable swamp of extraordinary dimensions which Mr. Oxley described as an ocean of reeds Here the expedition halted & this was the extent of the discovery the river run nearly in a western direction The next river explored was the Lackland whose source is about 80 miles from the former & both streams seemed to run nearly parellel with each other [T]he result of this expedition was similar to the first the river fell into an impenetrable morass & the party returned firmly believing that all the rivers of the western territory tended to the same point & that the central regions of Australia were occupied by a vast lake or inland sea This theory became established & it was a good while before another exploring expedition was thought of Not succeeding in finding a navigable river an attempt was made at making a better road over the blue mountains which was done but it was still so steep that drays were unloaded at the bottom & the contents taken up at several times Somewhere about 1826 I think it was Captain Sturt started with a party for the purpose of exploring the W & S.W. parts of the country & penetrating far beyond the morass which Mr. Oxley had stopped at they fell in with a river running somewhat to the South of West The land between the morass & this river is flat & bore evident marks of being flooded at times from which a conjecture prevailed that though Mr. Oxleys inland sea absorbed the waters of the Lackland & Macquarie when in their usual diminutive state yet that it was incapable of containing them when swollen by the rains which rush from the mountains At such times the lake seems to have run over & the water spread itself over a wide extended plain where the descent was so gradual that its motion was not enough to wash a channel I forget the exact distance between the lake & the river but I think it is upwards of 100 miles Capt. Sturt traced the Darling a long way till his provisions were getting short & he was obliged to prepare for a return without having accomplished the object so much wished for, namely a passage to the sea by water. The scenery along the banks of the river Capt. Sturt describes as not to be exceeded for gloominess & sterility the land he says is but slightly elevated above the sea & bears evident marks of a recent formation & must undergo another very great change before it can be applied to any useful purpose. In one part they travelled by the side of the river for three whole days over a hard callous soil without seeing a blade of grass a bird or a beast & all that gave relief to the monotony of the horizon was here & there a solitary cypress After this expeditions were frequent some under the auspices of government & others undertaken by private individuals [A]mong the latter was a very daring one performed by an enterprizing young man a native of the colony named Hamilton Hume who with one other man took their muskets & started off through the bush to the west bearing sometimes a little to the South & in this way they pushed along living on what they could shoot till they reached the sea at Bass Straits at a point not less than 500 miles from their starting place in a straight line In their journey they traced a river for many miles to which the name of Hume was given but persons who have followed in Subsequent years deny the existence of such a river without doubting Mr Humes statement but contend that it must be some part of the darling which runs very crooked & makes some extensive sweeps and bends Before this time some persons had found their way over the Mountains a great deal farther to the South & had formed Sheep & Cattle Stations in that direction. Here the tops of the mountains are so high that they are constantly covered with snow but on some of the lower hills it frequently melts & forms the source of another river which becomes a considerable stream & retains the name given to it by the blacks which is Murrenbidgee Its course is nearly west running almost parellel with the sea coast leaving a space between the ocean & the river varying from 150 to 400 [*miles*] according as the land & water encroach upon each other Settlements have been formed along the banks of the river as much as 200 miles & it have been traced far enough to find that it unites with the darling During my abode in the Colony Major Mitchell Surveyor General of the Colony went out three times on discovery & each time the object seemed to be to trace the darling to its termination but though I never saw the particulars of his last expedition I believe he failed in the accomplishment of his object I will here insert two paragraphs from Major Mitchells letter to the Colonial Secretary on his return rout from the second of the expeditions mentioned above It is dated "Camp, west of Harvy's Range Septr. 4th. 1835 The interior country west of the darling is diversified with detached groups of hills & low ranges broken into partitions resembling Islands but the general aspect thereof afforded no indication of its then having any water on its surface From 2 different hills each about 12 miles west of the darling & distant from each other about 70 miles I obtained extensive views across the country but from neither of these heights could I perceive any smoke or even any appearance of trees the whole country being covered with one kind of bush forming a thick scrub, with intervals rather more open but strewed with smaller bushes. During the 4 months just past no clouds gathered to any particular point of the horizon no rain has fallen neither has there been any dew &

the wind from the West & N West hot & parching seemed to blow over a region in which no humidity remained.

The darling did not in the course of 8 hundred miles receive a single river or chain of ponds on either side Such was the extent of the plains on its banks & the depth & absorbent quality of the soil that much of the water of high floods appear to be retained therein besides all the drainage from the back country Thus the springs appear to be supplied by which the river appears to be sustained by which the river is supplied during the present season of drought These absorbent plains extend to about 5 miles on an average from the river on either side hills of soft red sand bound them & reach about 3 miles further Undulations of deluvial gravel of a very hard silecious ? succeed & skirt the Base of the heights which generally consists of primary sandstone["] Such is the description given by Major Mitchell of the Darling & if it varies a little from Capt Sturts account you must know the river had a very long course & the descriptions relates to different parts In the same letter from which I have taken the above paragraphs Major Mitchell says the Darling did not contain more than enough water to drive an ordinary mill while others have spoken of it as a river in which a 74 gun ship might sail & both of these statements might be correct for all the rivers in the country seems to be subject to the like changes I have seen the one that passed by westwood when it was not more than six inches deep & I have known it to rise as high as 37 feet From these great variations & the consequences which they produce (of which I will inform you presently) I think it likely that no freshwater river will be found that is navigable The Darling it appears has a course of about 700 miles & yet at times it is almost dry I never could hear of anyone who had ever traced it quite to the sea when it drew towards that point the descriptions seem enveloped in a labyrinth The most correct statement appears to be that it falls into a salt lake 50 miles long and 40 broad & not more than 4 feet deep with a rocky bottom This lake is named Alexandria & it was supposed to discharge its waters into St Vincents Gulf but some Captain whose name I have forgot after examining the Gulf with great care denies the entrance of any river into it Then some persons imagined it might overflow & find another course similar to that which receives the Lackland & Macquarie while others think that as the waters are salt it has a subterraneous communication with the sea but its saltness is no criterion whereby to judge of its connection with the ocean for I have known deep holes of water in the creeks 40 miles inland that was almost as salt as brine In fact Capt. Sturt & others who have visited different parts of the world affirm that Australia in many respects possesses qualities peculiar to itself As there appeared but little prospect of finding a conveyance by water for the produce of the Colony to the west of the Blue Mountains the work of effecting a better road over them was set about in earnest about the year 1830 & before I left the country it was completed & a light coach carrying the mail used to run from Sydney to Bathurst (distance about 130 miles) every day. This road was made by iron gangs stationed there by government for that purpose. These are men who have been guilty of offences in that country after being transported from here & are sentenced to work in irons on the public roads for periods varying from three months to 5 years according to the enormity of their crime & their previous conduct They are formed into gangs of 70 or 80 & wear irons attached to both legs night as well as day while a guard of Soldiers stand by them with loaded muskets all the time they are at work which is about 10 hours each day exclusive of meal times Parties of this description were employed in lowering the rugged precipices & forming the above named road in doing which they had in many places to cut through the solid rocks. And from the nature of the work added to the deprivation of the free use of their limbs by the irons not a few I was informed lost their lives in the completion of the task which occupied several years & when finished was pronounced by some persons to be the greatest boon ever conferred upon the colony by convict labour. But bad roads in general & want of Navigable rivers will always be a drawback on the advancement & prosperity of the Colony

The rivers are nothing more than brooks or diminutive streams running in channels 50 & 60 feet deep with very steep banks Some of them seems to be supplied by springs which rise from the bed of the river: while others are wholly attendant on the rain that falls on the mountains & rush down to fill their channels. At all other times they are only a chain of ponds that is a succession of large deep holes full of water in some instances 2 miles apart & in others perhaps only a few hundred yards & a dry channel between them which is filled when it rains & gives to it the appearance of a river & even those that keep up a constant stream are very similar to a chain of ponds for there is in various places deep holes from 100 yards to $\frac{1}{2}$ a mile in length & some more where the water is 6 & 8 feet deep & so on to 20 while between these pools there is only a small dribbling stream of 3 or 4 inches in depth [B]ut the beds of the rivers being comprised of sand thse deep holes are subject to great changes as after a heavy flood you will frequently find the sand swept from the shallow parts & the deep holes filled up which makes it dangerous to cross in those places for a year or two as these new moved beds of sand are so loose that when a person gets into the middle of the river he will frequently sink all of a sudden up to his armpits & I knew two persons who narrowly escaped drowning in this way though there was not above 6 inches of water. One of these was the overseer of Westwood who was riding across when the horse sunk & he was thrown into the water but after a good deal of hard struggling himself & the horse managed to extricate themselves one on one side of the river & the other on its opposite bank & it was an hour or more before they come in contact with each other again The other person was an old man near 70 who was sunk so deep that he could but just keep his head above water & must have soon ceased to breathe had not some one most fortunately come by & released him from his perilous position. In some places for a good distance the beds of the rivers are rock and the water seldom more than a foot deep when at its usual low standard. In other places is to be seen masses of Timber which is brought down by the floods & at some bend of the stream the heads or roots of trees are driven into the soft sandy banks where they are fixed & others that follow get entangled in them till they form immense heaps through which young trees grow up & so make a wooden bank to the river About 4 miles below Westwood the Nepean runs through a mountain which actually appears as if rent asunder to form a passage for the water. At the foot of the mountain on the east side is a deep valley nearly in a line with the course of the river for ½ a mile above but a little before it reaches this spot it makes a sudden turn to the west then another short bend to the north where it forms two deep holes with a shelf of rock between them about 4 or 5 feet wide & not above a foot under water except in floods This forms a crossing place for persons on foot & horseback but it is too narrow for carts it is also dangerous for the former when there is a fresh as they call it that is a strong current after a little rain at which times it has proved fatal to many person who have had the hardihood to cross it[13] About a hundred yards below this shelf it enters the mountain where the channel is so narrow that the trees which grow out of the rocks on both sides mingle their branches A little within the chasm widens & through its whole distance (about a mile & a half) forms one of the most grand wonderful & picturesque sceneries that it is possible to imagine. It actually seems as though the mountain had been torn asunder by some convulsion of nature & the river invited that way out of its direct course to behold the mighty work it had performed & sport among its ruins The chasm from a little within its entrance throughout its whole distance of a Mile & a half maintains a tolerable uniformity of width which at the top I should guess to be about 300 yards.

I can hardly form any idea of its depth but this I know that when standing on the top the heads of very lofty trees that grow out of the crevices of the rocks near the edge of the water are so far beneath your feet as to appear like little shrubs. Though there is a plentiful sprinkling of trees and shrubs throughout you would wonder what could support them for not any earth is to be seen but from the bottom of the Channel to the mountain's top both sides present a wall of rocks such as the most skilfull artist could never imitate & such as strikingly demonstrates the superiority of nature (or rather natures great Author) over the works of Man. In some places the rocks project in others they recede in one part they appear firm & solid in another loose & ready to tumble & in fact at some former period thousands of tons have fell & laying in the bed of the river dams the water up which in pushing its way through the interstices & over the top roars & foams & forms a very beautiful cascade & this is the case in several places. In two or three places I saw immense masses larger than St. Pauls Church that were severed from the solid parts but arrested in their downward progress & leaving a Chasm a yard or two wide & so deep that the eye cannot penetrate to the bottom. In several places near the summit are large Caverns into 2 of which with considerable difficulty I descended when drawn aside the attention from the immensity & sublimity of the whole. I was not less gratified in viewing the beauties of nature on a more diminutive scale in these subterranean recesses the sides & roofs of which were of more exquisite workmanship than was ever performed by the Chisel & Mallet of the Mechanic. The stone is soft & sandy with veins of red, yellow, green, brown & some others winding & twisting in a thousand beautiful shapes & in many places much resembling in form the crankled yeast that works up on beer in a tub These caves wear every appearance of having been washed out by the water but if such was the case some great change must have taken place since the period of their formation for at the present time [*they are*] I should say more than 200 feet above the water at the time of the highest floods The rocks are too bold & rugged to admit of ascending or descending wholly in any place & the only means of access to the lower part is by the passage where the river enters or where it emerges from the mountain I have entered at the latter place & clambered from rock to rock & from tree to tree till I approached a considerable distance & gained a stone about as big as a moderate house which lay in the middle of the river & on it I sated myself about about half an hour & gazed with astonishment & delight at the irregular & massy cliffs rising one above another & towering to the very clouds while beneath my feet the stream was descending a rapid of about 40 yards in length & divided more than that number of times by fragments of rock that lay interspersed in its bed & which caused a considerable noise added to which there was a strong breeze rushing up the chasm at the time and shaking the trees & Shrubs that grew out of the rocks from the bottom to the top which sounded hoarse & hollow & seemed in this lonely abode to create a sort of melancholy but which was soon banished by considering the grandeur & Sublimity of the scene which at that time was heightened by the glossy leaves of the trees which seemed almost to peirce the blue vault of heaven & which were dancing & playing in the beams of the declining sun It is possible to proceed along the river from one end to the other of this chasm but to perform the mile & a half it requires 2 hours & hard work it is to accomplish it in that time I never went throughout myself but I have been along the margin at the top several times & I never visited this spot without admiring it more & more & parting from it with regret & with a desire to pay it another visit though it was more toilsome than my daily work for the side of the mountain is so steep in every direction that you cannot ascend in any other than a slanting & zigzag direction & in so doing you have in many places to climb over rocks with the aid of the branches of the trees or shrubs & in other places you labor along over your ancles in sand & from the steepness of the acclivity though you may raise your feet 12 or 14 inches you will most likely not gain more than 3 or 4 From the nature of the travelling you must be aware it is no easy task to gain the summit you are obliged to rest several times & even then after having completed the task my knees have trembled so that I could scarce stand up Here wether I went alone or with Company I always had a good long rest before proceeding any further & here is a most extensive view but like all other views in this country of any extent it is destitute of variety nothing is to be seen but a dense & gloomy forest as far as the eye can reach [T]he portion of the mountain that was cut off by the river on the eastern side is about a mile wide at the top in the broadest place & is level & covered with a deep soil to within about 100 yards of the river where it suddenly changes to rock which in some places for 50 or 60 yards square is a solid mass very level & presenting a surface almost as smooth as ice [I]n other places they are extremely rugged & divided by small & large chasm some of which we could leap over & others we were obliged to trace to their heads & go round them There are a great many places where you can approach to the brink of the precipice & cast a glance to the bottom of the yawning gulf & see here a broad expanse of smooth water & there a narrow heap of foam pouring over the rocks & through them but such is the depth that the sound from these cataracts is but just audible & if there is a little wind rustling in the trees you cannot hear it at all I have stood on some of these projecting points & gazed on the wild scenery till my brain became dizzy & I was forced to recede then rounding the head of the Creek or Chasm I have gained a similar situation at another point 100 or 200 yards from the former & looking back to it I have more than once observed that it have been an overhanging rock & so thin that had I known it before I should not have ventured on it from its apparent feebleness The thought would then come across me that probably the one I then stood on might be of the same description & I would immediately hasten from it & find some place where all was visibly solid before I ventured to take a fresh stand. In this way I have traced the river its whole length through the mountain both alone and with Company & neither myself nor those that went with me ever came away without being highly gratified with the scenery but I never had but one companion who went a second time the difficulty & fatigue of ascending the mountain overpowering their desire to explore the many curious phenomena it presents One time when I was there with 2 other men we rolled several large stones over the edge of the precipice (some of them should I think 2 hundred weight) & you can scarce imagine the noise & confusion that took place below as they often struck against the corners of projecting rocks beating off hugh masses whose additional weight acted with greater force on the next that came in its way so that by the time it reached the bottom it amounted to ten or a dozen times its original weight & the number of peices it is impossible to enumerate. Sometimes the stones would meet with no obstruction from the edge of the cliffs where we shoved them off till they descended (I should think) 150 or 200 feet & there dropping on a level shelf of rock they would be smashed into a 1000 peices & send up to the top a strong sulphury smell My head is not one of the best in the world to look down from such heights & after having been to this mountain I have laid on my bed & clenched my hands & shuddered at the thought of standing on such awful precipices far more than when I was there in reality The western portion of the mountain is much larger than that on the east side of the river in fact I do not know its limits in that direction but it extends about half a mile farther to the north & both sides bending round towards each other at the place where the water emerges forms a capacious basin of an oval shape about two thirds of which is surrounded by rocks of a similar description to those throughout the channel[14] [T]here is a vulgar belief that this basin has no bottom but of course an erroneous one the truth is that no bottom is visible though the water is very clear except when disturbed by floods: but that the water should be very deep is no wonder when we consider with what impetuosity it rushes out of its comparatively narrow channel through the mountains into this vortex [I]n time of high floods the force of the current is almost sufficient to tear up its bottom if it were solid rock: but the open side of the basin is composed of sand & probably its bottom too & then it is no wonder that it should be washed out very deep The water flows out of this basin through a very narrow opening & continues [*its*] course first nearly E and then N along a tract called the Irish Flats The channels of the rivers are in general very deep & sometimes after 2 or 3 days rain they are filled to the brim but it soon sinks again to its usual standard & it frequently happens that you see large trees 40 or 50 feet high lodged in the heads of trees that grow on its banks About 20 miles from Westwood is a place called Burrogowrang of which I used to hear a great deal & which I always felt a strong desire to visit but never had the opportunity Some of the men on our farm had been there among whom was the overseer & the following is the description they give of it It is a large plain surrounded on all sides by lofty and rugged mountains so steep that no cart or anything of the sort can ascend or descend. Through this plain runs a river the mountains being cleft asunder in a similar manner to the one I have attempted to describe above to let in & out. And the overseer told me that of all the frighful sceneries he ever witnessed that surpassed them all; the rocks in many places being perpendicular & measuring from the bed of the river to their summits one mile & a quarter these stupendous cliffs are of a blackish colour which enhances the Gloominess of the scenery The plain is one of the best for grass in the neighbourhood which induces many settlers to place their cattle there in spite of the difficulty of access to it & the innumerable caverns with which the mountains abound form such secure hiding places for bushrangers that cattle stealing is more prevalent than in almost any other place in the country so much so that if cattle happens to be missing two or three times in any particular district it is common to say that place will soon become as bad as Burrowgorang The people who have settled there never attempt to raise more grain than is necessary for themselves for if they did they could not get it away to any profit Their attention therefore is turned entirely to cattle as butter & cheese are articles which sell at a high price in general & this with great difficulty & labour they get up the mountains on the backs of horses and bullocks

I once went about eighteen miles from Westwood to the Southward and I seemed still as far as ever from those fertile & beautiful fields which I was told by the gardener at parramatta lay in this district of the country & when I complained that the country here as well as about Parramatta & Sydney seemed anything but fruitful they said it was certainly barren there but there was plains 100 or 200 miles farther up the country that was not exceeded in richness & beauty by the most luxuriant parts in England. These plains I never saw nor felt any anxiety to see for I set them down in my mind as no better than what I had seen & of this I was satisfied about 6 months before I left the country by a Shipmate of mine who called on me & who had spent upwards of

4 years in that part of the country & who assured me that it was if any difference inferior in beauty & fertility to the part in which I was living The face of the country for the 18 miles I have just mentioned was as follows the first 4 miles nearly level with a brown loomy soil in some places & in others hard & gray but the land rose very abruptly into high ranges of hills with deep & narrow valleys dividing them & continued about 6 miles farther These hills are comprized cheifly of small rough gravel & are clothed with a species of timber called Spotted Gum which seems to delight to grow in such situations as it attains an enormous size & height This tract is about 6 miles long & 3 wide & is divided into 7 or 8 parellel ranges by deep narrow valleys in the bottom of which & for a considerable distance up the sides there is frequently long green grass when the tops of the hills & the more level parts of the country are burnt up by the heat & drought There are many such tracts in the country & some of them of great extent & if in travelling your way should lay across them & the distance is 10 miles & to make a circuit round them should be 25 or 30 you would gain by choosing the latter rout for in descending in many places 50 or 60 yards together you must let yourself down by the shrubs & do not dare let go of one till you can make sure of another & when you reach the bottom it is often not more than 10 or 12 paces wide then you have to ascend in doing which the difficulty is as great if not greater than to descend as you must often crawl on all fours The tops of the ranges are in general equally narrow so that you are constantly rising or sinking and many of the valleys are 600 or 700 feet deep

But to return to my journey after passing these hills we came into a flat country of about 6 miles in extent where the soil was black & appeared deep but it lay mostly in a state of nature The other two miles of our journey was more hilly particularly at the extremity where was the commencement of the Burrowgorang mountains but it was past noon & I had 13 miles home so that time would not permit us to explore that curious place which from what I have heard of it cannot be fully accomplished under three days The object of my present journey was to see a Shipmate who lived at a farm called Montpillier laying on a hill among the deep creeks & gullies which for a considerable distance skirt the foot of the mountains[15] The land is very barren in this direction the settlers house the mens huts & the farm buildings were of the usual despicable description & in this instance were a pretty fair sample of the interior character of the place for the master was very poor & the men wretched. Such sceneries I know are anything but pleasant to a person possessing a heart that can feel for another but I certainly do wish you could just have one peek into such a one as that was The hovels into which a number of men are huddled together are in general (as I told you before) in many cases were in appearance worse than pigsties [S]till when they are well fed in that warm climate the house is not so much consequence & I have seen plenty who were cheerful in such abodes but when a very scanty supply of mean food are the concomitants of such dwellings with an equally scanty supply of bad clothing & this dealt out to men who are banished from their native country & from relations & friends it appears to me like the acme of human wretchedness Such was the situation of the men at the farm I am speaking of they had no meat butter cheese or vegetables but a little maize bread was their food & their drink what is called Scotch coffee that is the scraping of a cake that is burnt or bread burned on purpose & boiled in water I partook of a very little of this homely fare & in a short time took my departure as from a delay of 3 hours before I could find my shipmate who was gone to a neighbouring farm it was drawing towards 4 oclock & I had 18 miles home the last ten of which I knew I should have to go by myself as my companion & guide was a stockkeeper of [*my*] master's who resided at a cattle station at the head of the range of hills I spoke of in my journey up I come to that station the night before in company with him with some cattle so that we had walked but 8 miles that morning but I had to go all the way to Westwood that night so we walked on pretty brisk just calling on another Shipmate that lay in the way where I stayed but a few minutes but from what I learnt in that short time his situation seemed little if any better than the one I had just left I made but a short stay at the cattle station as the sun was drawing low & the remainder of my journey lay entirely through the bush & I had been there but once before The sun set while I was going along the range of hills but when I reached the point where I had to descend it was not dark & I could distinctly see Westwood farm (4 miles distant) & I observed that it was nearly under the moon which I took for my guide knowing she would not traverse far during the time I was walking that distance. The country before me was flat & thickly wooded but with so good a guide I knew I could not err much: so I descended the hill & found no difficulty in getting home where I arrived tired & hungry & never once felt a wish to go to Montpiller a second time About 2 years before this I went about 20 miles in an opposite direction to see a shipmate & another shipmate who lived near me went with me we went on a Saturday & returned the following day & my companion was so tired even at this rate of walking that I could never persuade him to accompany me again beyond a few miles The land throughout our journey presented a series of moderate hills with flat but not wide valleys & the whole of it appeared to be of the most sterile description There was a sort of road after the first five miles but what traffic there was on it you may guess when I tell you that we saw but three persons & one human habitation from the time we started till we got within 2 miles of our journeys end Here we crossed the Western Road as it is called that is the road from Sydney which goes over the Blue Mountains to Bathurst on both sides of which there were huts & we were glad to beg a little water from their inmates as the day had been a very hot [*one*] and we had found but one place where we could get any all the way & that out of a nasty hole & to [*make*] matters worse we were in many places assailed & tormented by swarms of large gray mosquitoes which we found it impossible to beat off effectively & their stings made my hands swell very much. From these huts we had 2 miles to go still through the bush but now without any beaten road or track but we went tolerable straight & found our Shipmate in pretty good health but low in spirits & badly situated His master was wealthy the house & farm buildings were pretty good for that country & he kept a great many men but he fed & clothed them badly much worse apparently than his dogs about 20 of which were running loose on the farm & they were all large & fat Here I may as well tell you that 20 dogs on a farm is by no means uncommon & in many instances the number is much greater & though in the case I have just referred to they were the property of the master I have known farms where they all belonged to the men On Westwood we had 19 at one time only two of which belonged to master. But the persons to whom they nominally belong have frequently nothing to feed them with so that they have to look out for themselves which they can do far better than they could here for on every farm the beef is killed for the use of the men so that there is a great deal of offal & then it seldom happens that a month passed & sometimes not a week without cattle dying in the bush when they can go and help themselves I think in many of the country parts that dogs are more numerous than men & even in Sydney the keeping of them had arrived to such a pitch as to attract the attention of the Legislature & an act of Council was passed to empower the constables to kill all the dogs found in the street without a collar with the owners name engraved on it & a reward was paid for the killing of each dog but I forget how much[16] [I]t was something considerable such as occasioned a sudden & formidable slaughter among the poor dogs & created an evil for the time worse than the one they sought to remedy for nothing was said in the Act about removing the dogs only to kill them & they laid about the streets in such quantities & in such a putrid state that great apprehensions were entertained that in that hot country they would produce some fatal distemper so that at last persons were hired (by whom I cannot say) to go through the streets & collect them together & draw them out of the town in cart loads. There is one remarkable circumstance attending these canine associates of men & that is not one of them was ever known to go mad though their progenitors were all originally imported from Europe & they are of a variety of kinds the same as in England & the colony has been established ever since 1788 And I heard it affirmed by one person that a mad dog was a thing never known in the Southern Hemisphere but whether that be correct or not I cannot say And now again to my Shipmates. We slept there on Saturday night & on Sunday Morning [*another arrived*] who lived about 2 miles from there so that there was now 4 of us the greatest number that ever met in the country when I was present After having a little talk about "old times" & showing each other our letters from England we started all together towards Westwood our companions we had been to see accompanying us about 4 miles on the road where we bid each other adieu. They returned to their respective homes (& I never saw them afterwards) & my friend & I proceeded on our journey home & I recollect aright we did not see a human being save ourselves till we came within about 2 miles of Shancamore where my companion lived We reached there a little before sunset & after having some refreshment I walked on to Westwood about 2 miles farther. I had now been 40 miles across the country from N to S & found no traces whatever of those beautiful fields & meadows which I was told abounded in this district. But I was rather more successful when I went 10 miles to the east where the country was opened for several miles round on the north bank of the river & the fields divided in the usual way with posts & rails but what I had seen nowhere else there was several farms in succession without any bush between them. This was the largest tract of cleared land I ever saw in the country I think it was about 3 miles long & a mile & a half wide exclusive of a piece that joined it at one end about ½ a mile wide and 2 miles long but of a curved shape so as not to be seen but a little bitt at a time The soil is deep & black towards the river & more shallow & brown as you recede from it but all capable of producing a good crop of grain when the season is kind. The South bank of the river is equally susceptible of cultivation but it is for a long distance the property of one person (or was during the life of the first owner who left it to his 2 sons) & is one among many of the original enormous grants from government to priveleged individuals it comprises a tract of 12000 acres a few hundred of which are cleared & cultivated & the rest lays in a state of nature on which are feeding in general about 16000 sheep This settler has about 100 men & sometimes more—on his farm including shepherds watchmen farm labourers & a few mechanics besides which he has two other sheep & cattle stations one about 80 miles & the other more than 200 miles at these places he has about 20000 more sheep besides abundance of cattle From such a number of sheep you must be aware that the yearly increase is prodigious & as the consumption of the country is inadequate to such an increase & as other settlers in general are stocked in proportion to their land I have heard it affirmed by many persons that in the lambing time they save only the best killing the rest & throwing them up in heaps by hundreds & burning them This I certainly beleive is done though I never saw it myself About 5 miles to the east of this farm is a town called Campbell Town which place I visited once & that was the limits of my travels to the east. The town consists of one street only running from the top to the bottom of a gentle hill about 800 yards long At the top is the church a tolerable handsome building standing a little from the road & on the opposite side is the Court house with the jail under it & almost joining it is a very good inn besides which there are several others in the place, but of an inferior description The three first named buildings are of brick & there are three pretty good private houses built of the same material & the remainder of the town is made up of weatherboarded houses & slab huts some covered with shingles & others with bark & mingled together in the most confused manner & fronting in almost every direction. At a short distance from the town on a hill stand the walls of what was intended to be a Catholic chapel the walls are about 12 or 14 feet high & at that thay had been standing for many years The land for several miles round is hilly & barren & seems to be a very incongrous situation to fix on for a township as water which is so necessary an article in town or village is very scarce & they have frequently to fetch it a distance of 6 miles from the Nepean When

I was there a shower had fell the day before & in a hollow by the side of the road a little way out of town were a few puddles out of which I saw a man filling a barrel that he had in a wheelbarrow though it was almost as thick as cream Such was Campbell Town when I saw it in 1834 but they talked then of building a dam across the valley to form a reservoir of water for the use of the inhabitants To the west of my abode the hand of civilization had made but little progress (& that little during my residence at Westwood) there was 2 farms on which was cleared about 200 acres of land Beyond this all was a solitary forest up to the foot of the Blue Mountains a distance I should think of 30 miles or more. Very little is known of this tract only that it abounds with deep & in many places impassable creeks which receive the waters from these mountains as also the Burrowgorang & Razor Back ranges. This is all I can say about the land for many miles round about Westwood as to the nature of the soil But in spite of every obstacle as to soil & climate the axe of the settler is yearly encroaching on the forest & during the 5½ years I was at Westwood there was about 700 acres of land divested of its natural burden within 3 miles of that farm & the two last years that I was there I saw crops of Indian Corn where the first summer I was in the country I went into the forest to see the blacks perform their dance called by them a Corroberee The following is the method which is found to answer best in clearing land the timber is cut down with axes about 3 feet from the ground in doing which every advantage is taken of the wind & the way in which the tree leans.

Sometimes a group of a dozen or twenty trees are all inclined one way when such is the case a notch is cut on both sides of the trees till you come to the last of the number or the one that stands at their head which being cut through falls against the next to it & beats that down & so on through the whole group & as the timber is in general large & lofty & most of it very brittle you would be surprised to hear the noise & see the confusion which ensue [W]here the timber grows very upright & the weather is calm the trees are cut more than halfway through & left in that state till there comes a wind which often rises very sudden & blows very strong & then down they go by dozens Whichever way it is performed the branches of the trees are in general very much smashed to pieces which is collected & piled in heaps upon the trunks at 10 or 12 feet apart & set on fire & if these fires are properly attended to they will burn the trunks off in lengths much easier & in less time than sawing them While this is going forward the spare time is occupied in clearing the earth of the stumps that are standing in the ground & cutting the roots partly through in which state they are left a month or two to dry when the trunks are rolled with levers into the holes around the stumps & some of the shortest of the peices of the branches which are reserved for the purpose is wedged into the open spaces & then the operation of firing commences again which requires to be attended to night & day to keep the logs rolled up to the stumps as fast as they burn away so that the latter may be burnt quite out of the ground deep enough for the plough to go clear but this oftentimes is not done

& many a plough is broke against the stumps after the land have undergone the process of what is called clearing The timber burns best when it has been fell about 6 months

I once witnessed a very pretty sight in going from Westwood to the cattle station of my masters over the high sharp ranges I spoke of in my journey to Montpellier I started early in the morning & there was a remarkably thick fog so thick that I could only see a few yards before me along the flat land for the first 4 miles. Soon after I began to ascend these steep ranges I perceived the mist somewhat thinner & its density gradually diminished till I got about 3 fourths of the way up where I found myself in a perfectly clear atmosphere & on reaching the top in the rays of the sun which was near an hour high & here beheld such a phenomenon such as I never beheld before or since & such as could not have failed to delight any lover of nature. The hills & valleys which had hitherto appeared in the distance as one unbroken mass were now perfectly distinguishable one from the other, the latter were filled with a thick fog which reflected the suns rays so powerfully that it dazzled my eyes to look on it & the high hills reared their heads above this mist & divided it into stripes varying in width & shape according to the valley I could not see the hills rise one above another from the place where I stood as far as the eye could reach also where a cross valley cut the ranges in two & where one range projected beyond another. And in many places where there was a broad sheet of white light there appeared a faint dark line which I took to be the tops of ranges of hills that were not sufficiently high to raise their heads quite above the mist [I] stood for a time almost unconscious of where I was going & gazed with astonishment & delight at the vastness & sublimity of the scenery around me then proceeding a few paces I took another stand & looking again & again till my heart throbbed & feelings arose which it is quite impossible for me to describe Everything around me seemed motionless & I was oft so too & the silence & solemnity of nature was only occasionly disturbed by the lowing of cattle which was heard far beneath that effulgent glare of humid light which seemed to present a solid & level surface broken only by the hills & spreading its mantle over the millions of acres of forest that lay to my right my left before and behind me. After taking a survey from various points & turnings of the hill which I passed I went on to my journeys end & when I returned in about 3 hours all the beauty of the scenery had vanished like the baseless fabric of a vision & nought remained [*but*] the monotonous view so common in all parts of the country

Bush Fires

THESE FIRES CHEIFLY occur in the summer months & rage as long as their is any fuel to feed them, unless arrested by a thunder shower or a general rain but the latter rarely descends in the summer. The causes are various by which the fire originates & the damage occasioned thereby is frequently considerable particularly when they happen before harvest or rather in the harvest as the wheat in the feilds not unusually becomes its victim Most of the settlers do not sow the headlands of their feilds but leave a border all round which they plough up & suffer to remain bare so that the fire may not run in upon the wheat this is a good precaution but not an effectual remedy as you will learn hereafter. The bush is often set on fire by the burning off of the timber in the manner I have before described. Sometimes the blacks set it on fire purposely to drive out the snakes, Bandacotes &c which they eat & which thus become an easier prey to them at other times they leave fires burning when they quit their camp & the wind blows it into the long grass & away it go in the most furious manner. Burning couch is also another means of occasioning these fires as the wind will often carry the fire to a great distance The hot ashes from a Tobacco pipe if dropped among the grass will set it on fire And I have no doubt (though I have never seen it) that it is sometimes occasioned by a flash of lightning by whatever cause it is ignited it is beyond all human powers to stop it once started Perhaps you may think that from the general aridity of the climate there can be but little grass to burn this certainly is the case in some parts & in some seasons but even where there is no more grass than on the downs of England in winter you would be astonished to see how the fire runs along you would think the very dust must burn as there appears but little else but the fact is the earth & air is so dry & hot that by the cattle constantly walking over the grass it is reduced to a powder & mingled with the dust But in many places there is great quantities of coarse rough grass of different kinds no better in quality than the sedge which grows on the margin of our rivers the tops only of which is cut off by the cattle & where the fire reaches these spots it roared again but still more so in some others These are deep valleys & creeks & sometimes the sides of hills which are clothed with a thick scrub among which grows quantities of fern & a sort of wild vine. I have stood near while the devouring element (driven by a hot & furious wind) have been making its way through a place of this description & the tremendous roar which proceeded therefrom actually seemed to shake the earth while the long bright tongues of fire streamed up far above the tops of the tall forest trees presenting the most terrific appearance. If you are in the bush & hear the fire approaching the best way is to seek a place where there is nothing but grass & that short & when the fire arrives at this spot put your hands before your eyes & run through it & then you are free from it as all is as bare behind as was the land of Egypt after the locust but if your road lay in the same direction that the fire is going you may proceed without exposing yourself to danger for though I have seen it travel with the speed of a horse at full galop it seldom continues this for more than 2 or 3 minutes in any one direction & when the fire is met by it it do not proceed half so fast as a man could walk In addition to the fuel I have already mentioned on which these fires feed there is the leaves of trees for though they are what is called evergreens yet they are constantly dropping their leaves one sort or another of them And then many of them shed their bark annually which roll up in curls & drop on the ground in strings from one to 6 feet in length so that with the leaves & this bark the surface of the ground is often covered shoe deep I have seen trees when the bark have been peeled off at the bottom of the trunk & at the end of the branches next the trunk while it adhered to the extremities so that the tree was hung round with more than a hundred ropes which continued for several weeks before they dropped Then there [*are*] the branches small & large that are continually falling from the trees as well as the trees themselves in every stage of dilapidation from the first symptoms of decay down to the hollow shell the decay mostly commencing at the heart & working outwards & I have seen shells 20 or 30 feet high & a little or no thicker than my hand with all the interior burnt out of them It sometimes happens that there is no general fire for 2 or 3 years & the abundance of fuel which accumulates in that time furnishes the stronger blase Such was the case when I first arrived in the country & as they had two moist seasons prior to that date there was a great quantity of coarse rouch [rough/couch] grass in many part of the bush which began to burn (from what cause I knew not) about 2 miles to the east of Westwood on the 8th. Nov^r.^ & it spread far & wide & continued burning till the 11th. Jany. following when we had a heavy & I believe a general rain which totally extinguished the fire & brought up a good supply of grass from the roots left in the ground During one week the fire was within a quarter of a mile of us & encircled us on 3 sides & many an hour first & last I have stood looking at [*it*] by night during which still & solemn period the scenery was inconceivably grand particularly when the fire is spread over a very large space such as it was the year I have just alluded to Most of the trees are hollow & many of them have their heads broken off 50 or 60 feet from the ground & when they have holes in them as is frequently the case the fire is almost sure to find its way to the inside which will ignite as quick as tinder & the flame ascend this natural chimney with the greatest impetuosity & pour out at [*the*] top in a stream 8 or 10 yards above the tree & oftentimes there are holes in the sides of the trunk where branches have been broken off & here the fire will shout for 2 or 3 yards so that in a dark night such trees as this wore a very noble appearance Then there are groups of stringy bark trees in some places the exterior bark of which is hollow rough & dry & the fire will run up them to the topmost branches in one minute just as if they were bound round with paper or straw but like these substances there is nothing to retain the fire & it dies away in a few minutes & the trees are left as black as ink. In many places there are large quantities of dead wood cow dung and various kinds of rubbish which are driven up in heaps by the floods & when the fire falls in with this by night the black curls of smoke which ascend in slow & majestic columns is rendered still more imposing by the brilliancy of the flames around In fact there is a grandeur mixed with awe attending these bush fires by night when ranging the valley the plain & the mountain which I cannot convey to you in any word that I am master of & so much did I like to gaze on them that I have got up in the night & walked out to feed my eyes with the treat & when every twinkling luminary in the wide arch of heaven have been obscured by clouds the light from the fire has been equal to the moon at a quarter old. And when all nature is wrapped in sleep & not a breath of wind is felt the smashing of the trees as they burn off & fall one after another & the loud echoes from the rocks & caverns resulting therefrom seemed to act their part in enhancing the solemnity of the scenery But there is a wide difference between looking at these fires by night & combatting with them by day which it have been my lot many times to experience but the largest & most difficult of which was the last summer I was there when the farm was in imminent danger of being burnt & must have been but for the road leading to & by it which was worn bare & which stopped the progress of the fire by presenting nothing whatever for them to feed on [T]hough for near half a mile from this road the land was clear & the grass short yet from the heat of the sun & the strenght of the parching winds the flames were pushed on so furiously that all our endeavours to stop it was ineffectual till they reached the road. The same summer also all hands had to leave the harvest feild several times to go into the bush to stop the fire that was proceeding directly toward [*it*] The means we employed was each man to get a good green bough & station ourselves in a line or otherwise (according to the shape the front of the fire presented) about 20 or 30 yards apart in a place where the grass was short & if possible where there was not much rubbish & when the fire approached this spot each man commence work & beat it back to where the next started from & then sweep the leaves back with his bough. This can be done pretty well by taking advantage of the time when the wind heads the fire & much better in the bush than on cleared land as the wind there blows more constantly in one direction [Y]et still the chances are I might say 10 to 1 in favour of the cleared band for every yard you extinguish there is generally so much gained whereas in the bush 10 or a dozen men might work till they almost drop from the effects of heat & smoke & after stopped a line of fire for a mile or so perhaps in half an hour have the mortification to see all their labour have been useless & that the fire is raging again as bad as ever. This is occasioned by the quantities of timber both standing & lying which take fire & from which the sparks & pieces of ignited bark are carried by the wind a long distance into the grass & wherever it drops it will light up again almost in a moment I have seen trees burst out in a flame near their tops when the fire have not been nearer than 40, 50 or perhaps 60 yards & in such cases it is all in vain to endeavour to put out the fire that is approaching for as the branches burn & the coals drop down on the rubbish the fire is sure to light up & spread afresh. When our wheatfields lie in the line of the fire all hands used to go a mile or so into the bush to meet it & after having stopped it in the way I have described we then returned to our work leaving two of our number to watch & put out if possible the spots that lit up anew but sometimes it would break out in a number of places at once & when they were thus overpowered they were to sound an alarm that we might go from the field to their assistance. When wheat or anything else is in danger we used always to beat out the fire in the evening & as the wind mostly abates with the decline of day & falls with the setting sun there is no fear of its breaking out afresh during the night & far back in the wild tracts where it is never controlled it burns very steady at that period. And oftentimes the next morning great heat and a universal calmness prevails till 9 or 10 oclock when all of a sudden you will hear at a great distance the most tremendous roar as if all the trees in the forest were waging war with each other & then you may prepare yourself for another combat with the fire. I never had a watch to note the exact time but I think I have known the wind to vary from 5 to 13 minutes in reaching us after we have heard the first signal of its approach. When it arrives it rouses up the fire that have been sleeping all night in the logs drives it among the rubbish ahead where it again commences its destructive operations while clouds of black smoke roll up in all directions filling the air & almost obscuring the ligh[t] of the sun Again in the evening when the wind abated the smoke would often appear quiescent above the tops of the trees covering for a time the whole face of the country & shutting out every object from view We often had three & sometimes four such days following but seldom more & then a few days of calm weather & once or twice I remember we had scarce any wind for a fortnight. During such time the fire slumbers waiting the next aid of its auxiliary to push it forward. This is the reason why the fire is so long in snaking its way through the country if the wind blew strong every day it would soon arrive at its journeys end. The fields (there indiscriminately called paddocks) are all divided by fences of posts and Rails & those who follow the business of fencing are pleased to see a strong fire making its way through the country as they expect to be benefitted thereby. And from all I heard it appeared there was never greater destruction made among the fences than by the fire of 1831–2 that is Nov$^{r.}$ Dec$^{r.}$ &

Jan[y.] many hundreds of miles being burnt down. But the fences are not the most material of the property that is oft destroyed whole feilds of wheat being frequently consumed & one small settler (about 8 miles from us) lost all in this way (not excepting his dwelling house & furniture such as it was) & went about the country with a paper expressive of the damage he had sustained & soliciting contributions to reinstate him in his business Another large settler within 3 miles of the same spot also suffered a great loss about the same time most of his wheat ricks & a great part of his farm building being destroyed the damage was estimated at 3000 pounds Nor are these occurences without their parellel in other parts of the country nay a more calamitious event than either of the above took place in the Hunter's River District where 2 children had strayed into the bush for the purpose it was supposed of hunting bandacoots & being so intent on their amusement did not perceive their danger & so became surrounded by the fire & fell victims to its rage. They were found some time after lying both together dreadfully burnt & quite dead You would pity the poor little animals & insects in advance of the fire trying to make their escape: a man told me he once saw 3 opossums run out of a hollow tree that had taken fire & ascend to the topmost branches where they sat trembling & an eagle hawk perceiving them dashed down & took away 2 [1] of them in his talons he knew not what became of the other two. You can scarce imagine a scene of greater desolation than presents itself in the bush after the fire has passed: hundreds of trees (green as well as dead ones) burnt down & smashed to peices some burnt off close to the ground & others at different heights up to 60 or 70 feet some of the tallest perhaps with 2 or 3 large extended arms which together with the trunks are all as black as soot & present a very ghastly appearance. All the leaves & small twigs are burnt off the brush or underwood where there is any & the principal stems left standing which with the bark of the trees the logs on the ground that are not consumed & the ground itself is all as black as ink & you will soon become the same colour if you have far to go The different kinds of wood differ much in the way of burning some of them the fire will not quit till it has consumed them & they continue burning for a fortnight or more while others soon go out

Thunder Storms

THESE STORMS OCCUR at all seasons of the year though most common in the summer months & the lightning is much more vivid & the thunder a great deal louder than what we experience in this country that is frequently but not at all times [B]ut though it is so voilent very few accidents occur therefrom which, next to the gracious dispensations of Him who "Delighteth in mercy & not in judgement" may be attributed to the wood of the country which it is said is highly impregnated with iron & therefore becomes a good conductor to the electric fluid & as most of the dwellings are built on cleared land the lightning is thus drawn from the habitations of man [T]he trees are struck in great numbers & broken in various shapes I have seen some of the loftiest & largest split from top to bottom sometimes rent off in the middle & shivered into a thousand splinters & sometimes the whole force of the lightning appears to have fell on the head of the tree & brought it to the ground just as you might take a heavy flat peice of wood & dash it down with your full strength on a small currant tree or any small tree or shrub. The clouds sometimes hangs so low that the thunder follows the lightning instantaneously & so loud & voilent & flies from side to side with such rapidity that I have seemingly felt its force on both sides of my head in a moment & for a time a sort of benumbing stupor have run through my whole frame & I remember setting on a stool in a hut during a tremendous storm when the sudden & furious manner in which the thunder burst produced an effect just as if I were lifted completely off the ground. The most terrific storm I knew while in the country (and many of "the old hands" said they scarce remembered its equal) was on the 19th. Febr$^{y.}$ 1832 from 7 in the evening till midnight. The lightning fell with such force on the ground that I fancied (but most probably it was a mistaken fancy) I could hear a sort of a whistling sound as it passed along Be that as it may the ducks & the geese that were loose in the yard darted & ran about when the streams of fire ran along just as if a fox or an eagle had darted in among them. The only damage done by this storm that I heard of was a chimney & part of a house beaten down in parramatta. There was great destruction among the trees in the bush but this was never considered as damage. But though there is a great deal of thunder at times yet storms of so violent a description are not very frequent I did not keep any account of their number but I should not think that they amounted to more than a score in our neighbourhood while I was there Sometimes they are attended with rain at others they pass off without any or perhaps a few heavy drops fall making spots on the dust as big as shillings. If it do commence raining at such a time it generally falls in torrents & so darkens the air that objects at a hundred yards distant are sometimes imperceptible Three of these voilent thunderstorms were attended with hail & anything more dismal you can scarce conceive Though they all occured in open day it was almost dark & the large hailstones &c poured down the bark & shingled roofs of the huts so furiously that the sound of the thunder was scarce audible only you could find the ground shake These 3 storms happened the first on Oct$^{r.}$ 8th. 1831: the second Feb$^{y.}$ 2nd. 1833 & the third April 7th. 1835 The deep scratches made by the hail in the shingles and fences in the storms of Feb$^{y.}$ 2nd were to be seen very plain 16 months after. It was almost like the hail in Egypt for it cut the Indian corn completely into ribbens and quite destroyed the melens cucumbers pumkins &c in the gardens. But such storms are very partial and seldom extend far the one in question did not exceed a mile wrath. A storm of this description in Nov$^{r.}$ 1832 which fell at Arthursleigh a farm of my masters about 80 miles from Westwood did great damage among the sheep many of them had one eye beaten out and some were quite blinded by it. And in a letter my brother sent me from Port Macquarie he informed me that there poultry was all killed by hail he went into the yard after the storm was over and found them dead and as flat as if they had been pressed beneath some heavy weight At a farm about eight miles from Westwood there fell some enormous hailstorms on Good Friday 1834 I think it was. I did not see them myself but a settler on whose veracity I could rely [as] well as my intimate frend shipmate Levi Brown assured me that they measured a great many that were 7 and 7½ inches in circumference and a few that were nine inches were not hailstones such as we see in general but irregular shated pieces of ice.[17] There is one thing worthy of notice relating to all heavy storms either with or without thunder and that is they settle invariably in the east or thereabout the most common spot being a little to the south of E. They cheifly rise in the N.W. though I have sometimes known them to come from other points varying from S.W to NE but I never remember one which terminated in any other direction than the one above mentioned. And lightning which is very common during the clear winter nights always proceed from the same point. In one solitary instant I saw it as near as I could guess about S.S.E. but never on the western side of south nor I think above t[w]o points to the north of east It is generally confined between E. and S.E and in that direction it is often very brilliant darting up into flashes faster than you can number them This mind relates to clear nights when storms are on the wing it illumines every point of the sphere in turn and assumes a thousand different shapes. I have seen it run along the horizon in the shape of a snake when in full-march and have obseved it burst from the dark cloud when realy vertical in a messy globe of light and branch in evry direction in fords [forks] and curls and evry shape you could mention

Sometimes these storms will continue flying about almost evry day for a month for a time and not rain enough fall during [*this*] period to lay the dust; And at other times in the hotest weather five or six weeks will pass without you hearing thunder. The most magnificint display of lightning I ever saw was on the 26th Jany 1834. It had been thundering all the afternoon and a little after sunset the dark clouds aling [*the*] western horizon gradually ascended and the lightning in escremely vivid flashes shone along the mountain tops in that direction and as the night closd in its brilliancy was enhanced. By about half past nine the clouds had reached an altitude of about 60 degrees and then a scenery commenced which would defy any human ha[n]d with pen or pencil justly to portray. The night was hot and a gloomy brethlessness seemed to pervade the terrestrial abodes. The lightning which had hitherto exhibited a ripid suscession of vivid flashes, was now no longer subjected [*to*] momentry ? but spread itself nearly from north to south over the greater portion of the western hemisphere in one magnificent sheet of quivering light behind which in awful majisty were ranged one above another huge columns of sable clouds over whose dark faces was constantly playing still brighter storms of the electric matter darting and flying in evry direction and terminating in brushy points much resembling the line of sparks which you undoubtedly have seen from a blacksmith George [forge].[18] The thunder was not of that violent description which I had often witnessed but was somewhat distant and rolled in heavy and long continued peals, with occasional thumps that caused the earth to vibrate The clouds and with them the lightning continued to ascend till 11 oclock when it reached the zenith. The overseer and myself stood in the yard viewing this brilliant phenemanon till that time when it became too powerfull for our eyes and we retired within doors and not minutes elapsed before a sudden guest of wind arose and blew with considerable strength for about ten minutes and then died away into a sullen calm. I went out again and found that the stars were shining very bright and nothing of the storm remained save few clouds in the east from which issued now and then a bright flash of lightning. The lightning of that night surpassed anything I ever saw before or since, and now that I am writing I seems to have it as fresh in my eye as when in the yard at Westwood on the night it occured

The Aborigines

THE ABORIGINES OF this vast region though deffering considerably in their dialect in parts remote from each other yet as far as I could see and from what I could hear appear to have spring from one common stock. Many conjectures have arisen as to the way and at what period they found an asylum in that country and also from whence they came. One commentater on the subject whose name I have forgot argues from the similarity of words made use of by them and some of the nations about Egypt in delineating the same article that they must have come from the [that] quarter.[19] They observe to my knowledge one custom enjoined upon the Israelites repeating [respecting] diseases but it might [*have*] originated among themselves and not have been borrowed from that people The law of Moses forbade persons infected with leprosy &c to come within the camp and this custom is rigidly of served [observed] by the blacks of N.S. Wales. They are very subject to scall heads and what means they apply for its cure in there wild state I cannot inform you but those among the settlements beg hogs lard which proves highly effacacious.[20] But while labering under the desease they are obliged to remain at a distance and are by no means allowed to come into the camp if the place and manner in which they assemble deserve that name. The north east cost of new south Wales is separated from the continent of Asia by islands and narrow channels and it is the opinion of some geographers that a neck, or portion of land once united these immense regions and that the Aborigines of N.S. Wales might by this means gain footting in that territory without having recours to the ocean. If such conjectures be correct the period of the great change which converted N S Wales into an island must I think have been very remote as numbers of its birds and beasts are unknown in any other parts of the world and in several other respects it pooses [possesses] properties peculiar to itself And as to the inhabitants if they came from Asia I should think they would have carried with them some of the principles of civilization such as were possessed by the nations of that continent in days of old but if they did all seems to have vanished with the exception of the custom above mentioned and whether that is to be regarded as a vestige of civilization or not is out of my power to determine At any rate if their ancesters carried with them any of the custom which characterize a civilized nation or [*not a*] number of generations must have passd away for those customs to have become so totally obliterated. They have no records nor do they appear to know anything of numbers beyond what is expressed by holding [*up*] one two or three fingers and so on They count by moons and will tell you such a thing happened so many moons ago holding up their fingers to denote how many but in this they cannot go beyond ten nor do I think that they are correct many times even under that number I have asked them how old a dog was which I should guess to be 7 or 8 years but they would give a shake of the head which seemed to imply that they could not answer that question Then I asked how many moons to which they would pois [point/push] up the whole of their fingers and let them down several times repeating at every elevation that many that many that many and so on from which it was clear that they could not tell any thing of their age They neither cultivate the smallest portion of land nor build them houses to live in nor is their any traces to prove that their ancestors did anything of the kind There is two spots of ground one about 30 miles to the south of any residence and the other on the bank of the Hunters River which I was informed by creditable witnesses as well as having seen the same in a book bears marks as if it had once undergone the opperation of ploughing The first of these lies in the road leading to the south of the colony and is always called the ploughed grounds. The blacks have been asked if they know what occasioned these spots [*of*] land to Assume their present shape but their are quite ignorant as to the cause Had any of their ancestors been acquainted with husbandry there certainly would have been more extensive marks of it remaining than these two spots of ground nor is it likely that the present race or rather generation should have so far retrograded from the path of industry as to possess not a single grain of corn an agricultural impliment, or the slightest notion of cultivating land. while I was in N. S. Wales I copied the following from an East India Magazine. "Australia— In the library of the Carthusian Friars at Evara there exists an authentic M.S. Atlas of all the countries in the world with richly illuminated maps made by Fernao Vaz Dourado cosmographer in Goa in 1570["] In one of the maps is laid down the northern costs of Australia with a note; "This coast was a hundred years before the Dutch had seen it who have since claimed the merit of the discovery["] Now, as these early voyagers were not sufficient acquanted with navigation to make much speed they were several years from home when out on discovery and as their ships were not built on so commodicus a scale a[*s*] though [those] of the present day [*they*] could not carry any great quantity of provision and I have read of their putting into harbours going on shore sowing grain and waiting to harvest in that way (if ever it was cultivated) then by the tricks of a navigable river is more likely. Some persons supposes the land to be formed into ridges by some great inundation in ages past but to such a supposition there is a strong objection for though the works of Nature are in mosty cases strikingly beautiful yet we seldom see her put work of that sort out of hand in so uniform a manner that have been done from all I have heard on the subject. I heard at one time that a burial place had been discovered on the western side of the Blue Mountain where the bodies were lain in rows in caverns and divided by stones which gave rise to an opinion that the country had once been inhabited by a more intelligent race of people that [than] the blacks are at present [B]ut as it [*was*] two years before I left the country and I searched every newspaper that I could come at, and made every enquiry I could without learning anything further about it, I imagine it was a false report or a story relating to some other land. Be all this as it may the blacks who are the present inhabitants of the county are nearly if not quite on a level with the brute creation They certainly are formed into ? tribes and have some customs resembling laws among them. Each tribe has its tract of country and its boundry set and goes by a particular names as the Ilawarra tribe the Burrow-Burrow the Bong-Bong the Woollindilla and so on They have also a sort of superior or Chief over each tribe but I believe the principal distinction between him and the rest of the tribe in thir wild state is that he is allowed two Gins (women[)] while they are confined to one. Most of those chiefs among the settlements wear a brass plate in the shop of a half moon suspended from their necks with their names engraved on it which is given to them by some of the settlers and of which they appear to be very proud Sometimes one tribe pays a friendly visit to another which is celibrated with a dance called by them a corroberee: but those dances are sometimes performed by one tribe only and none but the young men engaged in it the older ones contenting themselves with looking on and now and then issuing a show of opprobation while the young woman sit on the ground with their oppossum skin cloaks rolled up in the shape of a ball and laid in their laps which they beat with ther hands; the dancers have also a stick in each hand which they beat to gether and both make a strong though not very harmonious sort of singing noise in which they seem to display some little knowledge of sounds as they rise and sink their voices in unison but when you have heard them about one minute you are acquainted with all they are capable of performing in this way for if they keep on for 2 or three hours which they frequently do with the exception of short pouses [pauses] it is the same sound over and over again and again. The same irksom monotony attends their dancing also for though the[*y*] display the most admirable dexterity in the use of their legs yet the number of their evolutions is so small that ones patience becomes exhausted in about an hour in looking at them I went twice to see them exhibit and the manner in which they dance was conducted was as follow:—the dancers are naked with the exception of two small things which I cannot give a name to but they are made of the fur of the oppossum spun into ringlets much like the twists of wool of which a map [mat] is composed only smaller [A] number of these are strung together till it amounts to size to that of a small horses tail and is about 18 inches in length A belt is fastened round the waist and one of these things suspended from it before and sometimes (but not always) one behind. The[*y*] use pipeclay with which they stripe themselves from head to foot in various shapes, which contrast very strikingly with their black skin and gives them a wild and savage appearance. The dance is mostly performed when the moon is near the full so as to have a strong light but when this is wanting they make a large fire near which they arrange themselves in a row and commence singing and moving about in an irregular manner for a time then suddenly advansing towards each other they from themselves in to a huddle raising their voices to the highest pitch and jumping violently on the ground and ending abruptly with a loud shril whoop after which they whirl themselves round and seperate After a short pousd [pause] they again form into a row at some distance apart each one extending his feet to the distance of about three feet in which attitude they all jump together accompanying the sound of their feet on the ground with a loud eagh or grunt something like an Irishman when using a heavy rammer or pitchen. And though they do not bend [*the*] joint of the leg they shake them from the heel to the hip in a most singler and wonderful manner. When they have exercised themselves in this way for a few minutes the dance ends much the same as the first In the next dance they all squat down putting their hands under their thighs and jump after one another in a circle giving utterance at each motion to the same sound as in the last dance. This attitude in jumping is I believe in imitating of the kangaroo I believe I have now enumerated all the evolutions they go through and if you stand looking at them for three or four hours you become wearied with the insipid sameness which pervades the whole of the performance. I went twice to see them and had no desire to go any more though I have frequently heard them their noise being carried on the still spot [hot] air of the night to a great distance and they never dance by day They sometimes meet in a more hostile manner which is mostly occasioned by one tribe stealing a woman from another. I never saw one of these meetings but it has been thus described to me [T]he belligerant tribes draw near to each other and the woman of the aggrieved party advance within hearing of the aggressors and demand a restoration of the captial [captive] if this request is complied with the affair is brought to an issue but if not a challenge [*of*] physical strength is made also by the woman and the females of the opposite party bids them defeance and after a good deal of jabbering on both sides the man advance to the combat which is carried on for a time by throwing spears and bumrings (wooden swords) [boomerangs] till at last they come to close quarters and fight with their nolla nollas [T]his is a heavy club about two foot long with a heavy large head and oftentimes carved in a curious manner In these wars though the wounded are numerous the amount of killed is but small The fate of the captive female depends on the result of the contest It sometimes happens that a man takes away anothers woman in the same tribe in which case he is sentenced to have a certain number of spears thrown at him but he is allowed his heeliman (shield) to defend himself [T]his is but a very narrow impliment but so quick is their eye and so agile are they in the management of it that they seldom let a spear touch them. If the woman is the faulty person she is subjected to a severe beating with sticks. The men in stature are about the middle size some few but very few rather handsomely growed but the majority of them have remarkably small straight legs quite destitute of a calf Their dress consists of an oppossum skin cloak or a blanket in winter drawn tight round the neck and hanging loose over the body reaching about midway between the hip and knee and in summer they have often nothing more than these things I described to you as worn by the dances The women are short and remarkably shall [small] with legs less in proportion that [than] of the men so that they actually look no larger that [than] map stick [matchstick] Very few of them have pleasing features and numbers of them are even offensive and rendered completely loathsom by the filth in which they are enveloved and was it not that I deemed it on insult to the Deity to apply the word ugly to any part of his handy works I should make use of it in describeing these women Their dress is the same as the mens only that in the summer fewer of them are to be seen without cloaks or blankets The children at that season both meal and female go quite naked The tribes among the settlements rove about from one farm to another begging bread, tea sugar tobaco and meat when they can get any fresh beet[beef] salt meat they will not eat. Their wants above what they can beg is supplied by catching and roasting small animals and fish but so completely are they overpowered by laziness that they will not exert themselves to procure anything by hunting while they can make a shift to live on what they beg They sleep in the bush without either hut or tent having only a few bough stuck into the ground at their heads and a small fire at their feet. The tribe is divided into families each of which sleep seperate so that they have sometimes from 10 to 20 fires. When rain comes (which is but seldom) they strip sheets [*of*] bark from the trees and sometimes put forkid sticks into the ground so as to form a quarter of a circle and lay sticks in the forks on which they lodge one end of the bark and rest the other on the ground [A]t other times I have known them to cut each sheet of bark crossways in the middle to make them bind free [bend freely] and then place both ends on the ground so as to form the letter A all but the stroke across it but the former way makes the most commodious hut. Should it rain three days which is sometimes the case when it do set in they will not stir from these hovels during that time and when they do turn [*out*] they are so hungry that they begin to hunt and beg in ernest and are not very nice about cooking [I]n fact cooking is an art in which they seem to have attended [attained] but little knowledge for when they catch an oppossum if they do not want the skin they will throw it on their fire and cover it over with ashes or coals for a few minutes then take it of and [h]old it hight with one hand and rub it down with the other which takes all the fur off and leaves it as white as a scalded pig they then tear open the belly with their fingers and pull out the entrails with a dexterity and facility which you would scarce believe without ocular proof. This short description is sufficient to convey to you a knowledge of the whole of their cooking for wether they have beast bird or fish it is all put over or under the fire just as it is caught where it remains only just long enough to scorch the outside After this the application of all its parts is of the most disgusting description the animal being torn apart with the hands and devoured without form or ceremony the blood and juice running out of their mouths and down their chins while entrails (if they are not so hungry as to [*word missing*] them for food) are placed in the hollow of the hand by which they are conveyed to the crown of the head and rubbed into the hair which it [is] thick and curley and so clotted with blood and greace and dust that they resemble an exceedingly dirty mopThe women are not allowed to eat any till the men have first satisfied themselves and if their is nothing left they must go and hunt for themselves and when all other sources fail it is no uncommon thing to see them with a flat sharp stick made for the purpose, dig up an ant hill placing it on a sheet of bark and shaking it forward and backward to seperate the ants from the eggs [W]hen they can get rid of the former they are not very nice about cleaning all the dirt from the latter but roll up eggs and dirt thogether into balls with a little stringy bark and with this they satisfy the cravings of nature This dainty morsal I never saw prepared but the men on our farm who witnessed it told me how it was done and the paddles with which they dig up the ants I have frequently seen as the women carry them about with them In the summer I have known the tribes to come to Westwood nearly all of them without clothing and doubed doubed all over with red clay this some of them will tell you is a token [*of*] regret for some deceased friend in their tribe while others say they only do it to keep themselves cool I cannot say why it is but I have observed in many instances that they seem extreamely cautious in giving satisfactory answers to enquiries while at other times they appear pleased to give all the information they can This mode of life being so repugnant to anything you ever witnessed as well as to the general method of living in England you might be almost led to suspect me of exaggeration but I assure you the statements are facts as far as I have seen and what I have related that have not come under my own observation so well corresponds with what I have seen that I doubt not of its truth And I assure you that these blacks from their habits of extream filthiness both externally and internally are productive of such disagreeable obours in hot weather that if your olfactory member but [be] not deprived of its function, you need no ocular testimony of their proximity when you are to the leeward of them. They are very dexterous in climbing trees in search of oppossums which live in the hollow parts and are about the size of a rabbit. The method the[*y*] use in ascending is as follow;—they cut notches through the bark which in general is pretty thick and just penetrate the wood; the notches are cut in a zig zag direction one for the right hand and one for the left, and about two feet above each other. Their toes follow their fingers in the notches and a very few minutes is sufficient for them to reach the branches of the talest tree which is sometimes 80 feet They descend with either [even] greater celerity [*than*] they go up as they have not then the notches to cut though that occupied them but a very short time [W]hen working in the bush one day I saw a black go up a tree so I though[*t*] I would look in a minute or two and see if he found an oppossum and when I turned my eye that way he was down and had almost reached the top of another tall tree and I then kept my eye on him and observed that after he got among the branches he broak off a dead stick to probe a hole in order to custom [question?] if they where an oppossum in it but the stick being too long for his purpose he stood erect on a large bough that proceeded from the trunk in a horizental direction and elevating both hands at arms length with the stick in both he brought it down on his crown of his head with a sudden jerk that snapped it asunder the stick was then applied to the hole but without succes and he soon after descended. The branch on which he stood was I think about 60 feet from the ground, and the blow on the head almost sufficient to have knocked some person down but I have been told by those who have anatomised then that their skull is more than double the thickness of an Europeans. They will seldom go up a tree the second time without cutting fresh notches unless it be within so short a time that the old ones are not warped by the heat. The women will climb as well as the men but I think in general they do not ascend very high trees. Sometimes they cut the oppossums out of hollow logs that are laying on the ground, and should he chance to run out before thay can lay their hands on him they will raise their arm with the tomahawk taking a cool and deliberate aim, and are sure to hit him in his retreat, as the best gunner in England is to kill a hare when running. The tomahawk is a small axe similar to those used by a hurdler and is given to them by government and the settlers; before whose arrival in the country,, they used flat stones made sharp (one of which I have brought home with me) and twisted a withe round it in the same way that blacksmiths do round their chisels punches &c. The bumring (wooden sword) which I mentioned before is in shape like the felloe of a large wheel only that perhaps it do not bend quite so much; its length about 2½ feet, its breadth two inches thickest in the midde and sharp at both edges, and the skill the blacks desplay in throwing this implement is past the imitation of any European. Many times I have stood and gazed with amazement and delight at the performance. The overseer used to give some of them sugar and tobacco at times on purpose for them to throw these bumrings which they do in a way that astonishes every beholder. They throw it straight forward as any person might a stone when it soon attains a revolving motion which increases till its velosity is so great that it looks like a circle in the air as it gradually ascends and makes a loud whizzing noise which becomes more and more faint till it quite dies away in the distance as do the circle to the vision when the when the bumring is is thrown by a strong man. For [*a*] few seconds you will again see it plainly on it return and in a little time the sound revives and [*the*] weapon granually appraxemates the person who threw it till at last it dropped near his feet or twenty or thirty yards from him. It mostly comes to the ground and [in a] steady and gradual descent but I have several times seen it become stationery at 10 or 12 yards from the ground and run round in a horizantal direction for several seconds with the velocity of a mill stone then suddenly drop like a bird that is shot dead. When on its return they apear to know where it will fall for some of the men when they saw it apprsaxhing [approaching] have run away when they would call out bale it come there (bale means no but often sounds singular as used with there broken English) At other times when persons standing by thought there was no danger the blacks would call to them to take care of there coberas (heards) [heads] and the bumring awalys [always] fell as their words seemed to indicate. The space it traverses do not amount to quite half a circle for when thrown to the N.E. it mostly come back from the W. or perhaps a little to the N. of W. In addition to the manner of throwing I have mentioned I have seen them pitch the bumring on the ground at 10 or 15 yards from then after which It would rise as before and I have seen them throw it so as to skim along the surface of the ground for about 200 yards and you would think every moment that it must strike and turning round so steadily as not to form perhaps more than ten revolutions in that distance then increasing its vecloity and gradually rising, it would attain as great [*height as*] an implement called [could] thrown either of the other ways and come round in the same manner. They can throw it also with the wind or against it and it makes no difference to its coming back they are also as expert in throwing their spears as they are in throwing the bumring and it is far more bentficial to them as they often kill beast and birds with it while the latter seems used chierfly for amusement or in hostile engagements. In throwing the spear they use an implement called a womra which is about 3½ foot long with a hollow hole at the extream point in which the spear lies and rests along the handle which is very narrow and has a gag at the end with a fine point to fit into a small hole in the end of the spear. The spear is laid into the womra and the right hand elivated and hold back considerably behind the shoulder with the fore finger over the spear to prevent it from slipping out of its place the left hand is employed in holding up the front of the womra to give the required elevation to the spear In this attitude the[y] stand to take aim at any object and then being [bring] the right hand violently forward with an inclinitating of the lady to give it force. In this way the spear is thrown to a great distance and the womra left in the hand. I have known them throw their spears on our farm in the same way that they did their bumrings but never saw them take aim at a mark though I have been informed by those who have witnessed it that such is the deliberation and precision which they display in the performance that they no[*t*] unfrequently kill a bird on the top of a tree or pirch [pierce] a duck through as its on the water. The spears are made in two parts the staf or handle being of an exceedingly light wood called grass tree, and about 7 or 8 feet in length The points are about 2 feet long and made of iron bark, a wood that is very heavy and extreamly hard; the two parts are made to fit very nicely and bound together with the fibers of [*a*] very tough sort of wild vine called by them curry jung and the joint strengthened by rubbing it over with gum which they get from the gum tree and is of a very adhesive quality. They polish the joint and make it smooth and neat. The heads of some of their spears is round and brought off gradually to a very fine point while others are flat with curved barbs down one side which are pointed with a substance resembling glass cemented to the wood with gum The points are very sharp and the spear has a formidable appearance. The blacks possess the faculty of smelling in a very high degree a[nd] will trace a white person (and probably one of their own party) with a[*s*] great accually [accuracy] as a pack of hounds will follow a hare; by which means many a robbery have been discovered. They seem cautious in letting any one know whether it it is by vision are [or] smell that they are gifted with the means of pursuit, but I think there is little doubt of it being the latter, as they will trace a person over a mile of smooth rock were there is not a article of hearth [heath] and, consequently where the human foot can leave no impression. Our overseer in riding over a paddock of 700 acres after some cattle lost the key of the store out of his pocket and he wished to try a black fellow, as they call themselves to see if he could trace the horse and find the key but he could not meet with any till the next day and they said bale it any good then and added, that had they been there at the time they should have been sure to find it for him Now if it was by sight that they followed I should have thought that one day would not have made so much difference, as the horses prints if he made any would not have been effaced in that time. In short such is the parched nature of the soil in general that no impression is left either by men o[*r*] beast [B]esides what would render the task of pursuit more difficult is that the earth is for miles together in the bush covered over with dry grass dead leaves and bark which I think must entirely deprive the most quick sighted being in the world of all power of tracing by marks. But be it as it may it is a fact beyond dispute that they will follow a person across roads over rocks and through many intricate windings to the place of their retreat, with a precision that is truly astonishing. About two years before I left the country cushrangers [bushrangers] short [shot] a constable about 20 miles from us and some of the neighbours having gained information as to the destruction [direction] the murderers had taken got some blacks and commenced the pursuit when after a hunt of several miles through the bush are [one] of the blacks laid down on the ground for several seconds and on getting up exclaimed bale croppy far off now and in a few minutes they came up with and took two of the men by the side of a river. This is only one among many instance in which they had been instrumental in the capture of persons who have been guilty a [of] offences. But every means hitherto employed [*to*] bring them to habits of industry have proved ineffectual. One large settler set apart a portion of land for the use of the tribe in his district and furnished them with the necessary seed and implements for carrying on cultivation while he solected the most intelligent of the party to be their chief manager but they could not be induced to work and the scheme consequently failed. In the infancy of the Colony a building was erected for a school wherein to enducate the childeren and many of both sexes where brought up within its walls where they where taught to read and write and the femals in particular where instructed in needlework and household affairs in generally in order to make them fit companions for white men who could contract a matrimonial attainance [alliance] with them and who received some immunities from Government for so doing in the way of land husbandry utensils cattle, and such like.[21] Most if not all of the women who were thus disposed of left their husbands and their homes, and perpetuated the custom of their ancestors by living a roving life in the forest. But I have heard it hinted that a very prominent cause existed for their so doing beyond that of their innate propensities; and that was, ill treatment on the part of the husband, who but too frequently married them for the property attached to the union and then abused them to drive them away. As these things occurred many years ago of course I can only relate them to you as I had them from others but be they correct or otherwise, one instance come within my own observation which favours the opinion that the wandering life is stamped in their nature. A tawny boy whose father it was said was a white man on a large estate about 10 miles from Westwood was taken by the proprietor of that estate and put to assist the man in the stable, and clean knives and shoes, and such like; where he continued for two or three years and seemed quite handy at his work: he used to go in errands as well as work about the home, and I have known him to come to Westwood on horseback with letters to the overseers. Well some time after I saw him along with one of the wandering tribes that came to our overseer to beg some Indian corn and who stated that they were murry wiaroo (very hungry). He continued with the tribe for a long time, at least for many months, after which the settler got him back again and he remained in his place during my time in the country, but whether ultimately he will choose the farm, or the forest for his abode of course I cannot determine. There were two more boys similarly situated with settlers, nearer Westwood than the one I have mentioned, but though I have seen them both; I know but little about them though from what I could learn they where sometimes absent from the farms for a time and would then come back again. Whatever ultimately may be achieved in the way of civilizing them little or nothing can be said to be done at present, and they must be very hungry if they perform the most trifling work for victuals. I have known them to husk a little Indian corn for some flour, sugar, or tobacco, and even them [then] the men will not often put their hands to it, but stand by and make the women do it: and if you give the stipulated articles, or any part of them, before the work you assign them is compleated you may rest assured that will not be done. I have known the overseer at Westwood to give them some wheat at times that they might grind it in the steel mill; but if the weather was hot, they would go away and leave it, being too laizy to turn the mill and denouncing the wheat with a valgar expressions they have learned from their white neighbours, and saying that they wanted plour (flour). Their is one Church Missionary employed to introduce among them the principles of Christianity. He is stationed at a remote part of the Colony to the westward called Wellington Valley, and was during my residence in the country accused by Dr. Lang a Scotch Minister of being an untrustworth[*y*] man together with some other epithets calculated to injure his caracter and which was the subject of legal proceedings in Sydney wherein the Missionary obtained a verdict together with daingers [damages] of one farthing.[22] His own account of the success of his labours in his capicity of missionary is no[*t*] of a very encouraging nature for though some of the blacks seem to listen to him attentively for a time, he cannot persuade them to stop at the station constaintly so much are they addicted to a roving life: and he cannot stale [state] satisfactoraly that he have made one real convert. A mode of procedure was adopted for their destruction in the yearly days of the Colony which proved more effectual than the means hitherto employed to convert them to Christianity. They killed two or three persons on an estate about 10 miles from Westwood, and I believe one or two in another direction and had these murders been traced to their origin, probably the fault would have been found to rest with the white men rather than the blacks for in addition to their feeling themselves aggrieved at the white people setting down as they call it in their land, the[*y*] are often further exasperated by their new neighbours takeing away their women and when thus provoked they gave full scope to the spirit of revenge, which I believe is nothing but what is common to all savages. For these murders martial law was proclaimed against them and they were slaughtered without mercy wherever they were found. About 15 miles from Westwood is a place still known by the name of the ["]Soldiers flat", where a party of militray were stationed to scour the bush and shoot as many as they could find of the unfortunate aborigines; and this severity I believe was practiced during the administration of one who bore the dignified appellation of "The philanthropic Governor".[23] Nor are these benighted wanderers in a much better case at the present time in the interior where many of them or [are] shot by shepherds and stockeepers with as little ceremony as the[*y*] would shoot one of the native dogs that come to prey on the flocks. My master had sheep and cattle stations on the Murrenbidge River about 300 miles from Sydney and one of the stockeepers when he brought down some cattle stopped several days at Westwood where I heard him relate their exploits in destroying the blacks seemingly with as much pleasure as if he had been relating a hunting excursion. I said to him, why you must be joking, you dont kill them do you. Certainly he said, our lives are in dainger, and would you not sooner kill them, then [than] let them kill you. I made no reply as I was satisfied any thing I could have said in favor of the blacks would have [*been*] quite useless so I did not again intrrupt him in his narritive as I know not how I might have acted in such a situation myself; but this I know, that I never could have exulted in their destruction if in the preservation of my own life I had been compelled to resort to such inhuman means. The [He] said there was one to whome the white men had given the name of Major, and knowing him to be a treacherous man they whatched their oppertunity one day when he was alone and shot him and rolled him down the steep bank into the river and the next morning fearing that his tribe would miss him and come that way and [in] serch of him he went down to the river to see weather he were still their when he found him lodged in the head of a tree that had fallen into the water so he got a long pole and shoved him out further out into the stream that he might swim away. His companions came and enquired for him and would never be throughly persuaded that they (the shepherds and stockman) know nothing of him. He said that during his residence at the station (two years) there was seven blacks killed by them and some of their neighbours. These murders are not sanctioned by Government but the case stands thus:—many of the settlers whose cattle and sheep had increased beyond their mearns of support on their origanal farms sent part of them into the interior beyond the boundary of the Colony. A number of persons in humbler circumstances who had reserved their ways [wages] in cattle and which had increased in some instances to from 20 or 30 did the same, and all these are termed squatters and this line of proceedure gave such facility to that dishonest population to steal cattle and take them into [*the*] interior and form settlement of their own that many of the most wealthy individuals in the Colony made complaints to the authorities in Sydney on the subject who took cognization where [*it was*] to be carried on yet all the waste land between that line and the eastern limits of the South Australia were to be considered as the property of Government, and no one was to settle without a liceance and the payment of a quit Rent so that every one of good character were obliged to retire within the limits of the Colony.[24] But the wealthy settlers are stretching further and further every year and their flocks and herds are becoming exceedingly numerous, requiring a great number of men to attend them. In this situation, past the limits of the Colony Government affords them no protection; and the blacks savage as they are, are still not totally devoid of patriotism, and fell [feel] repugnant to the proceedings of those postaral [pastoral] gentleman and being often otherwise provoked the[*y*] commit at times depredations among both men and cattle; which probably would not be the case if their were soldiers at hands to intimidate them, for they are exceedingly frightened at soldiers. But as the matter stands at preasent there is constant warfare between blacks and whites. Some have affirmed that they evinced a favourable disposition towards their white neighbours and are glad when they settle among them but such is not the case in general, an opposit feeling manifesting itself in an ? which they make as soon as they can speak English plain enough to be understood; which is, "What for white fellows come and sit down on our land"? To which interrogation a taunting and uncoth reply is often made as follow; "Go along with you, you black b----r.["] Even in the settlements were blacks and whites are on more friendly terms, and the former receive a great deal of food from the latter, they do not like some of the proceedings of the white men It is a custom with the men on some of the farms to go out with guns on moon light nights to shoot oppussoms in the trees for amusement and some times they sell the skins to the hatters in Sydney for three shillings a dozen. This is a thing which the blacks cannot approve of and they are not scrupulous in telling you so. One night our men was out on an excursion of this kind when the[*y*] fell in with a camp of blacks, and invited them to go along with them to which two or three assented and though they are much quicker sighted in general than white men yet they would not see one oppossum; and when the men fancied they could see them in the trees and were further led to believe they were there, from the manner of their dogs, the blacks would sternly protest that they were mistaken, and say, "Bale any possum there I tell you". This I believe is nearly or quite all the information I can give you relating to the wandering tribes of N.S. Wales.

Beasts

THE SORTS OF beasts seems not to be very numerous; thoug probably there are many with which I was not acquainted. The following I think is all that inhabit the parts I have been in; that is, the kangaroo wild dog, oppossum, bandicote, wild cat, wombat, squarrel, flying fox guano, and mouse. The kangaroos sometimes go in large flocks, of an hundred or more, and are sometimes to be seen singly. You have most likely seen them in shows and therefore need no discription of the animal but you would be surprised to see them bounding along on their hind legs and tail, clearing 15 and 18 feet at a leap and they have been known to make a spring of 22 feet. It is a droll sight I assure you for I think that they are four or five feet from the ground in the middle of their leap. There is four distinct species of them, the largest about 5½ feet in hight and the smallest not much larger than an English hare the other two sorts are in regular [*word missing*] between these. The first are called kangaroos the second wallobies the third fliers and the fourth kangaroo rats. The wild dogs called native dogs are sometimes larger than a fox coarser in the limbs and altogether stronger built. They are mostly of a [red]ish or a rusty colour though now and then one is to be seen that is nearly black. They sometimes go about in droves of eight or ten, and sometimes singly they are extreamly voracious and if taken when a few weeks old, and bread up in a house or hut so as to be as tame as the other dogs on the farm, they still retain so much of their savege nature that they can never be kept from killing geese, turkeys, ducks, and any thing that come within their reach. The settlers are obliged to have watchman to guard their sheep by night, and even with this precaution it not unfrequently happens that great destruction is made among them by these native dogs I once knew four of them to attact a calf of a year old, but rather small for that age. It was soon after day break, when I heard the bellowing of a calf and guessing what was the cause I got up and run to the spot as quick as I could (a distance of about three hundred yards) where I found the calf laying on the ground, and four native dogs tearing it in the most merciless manner; two of them decamped when I approached within a hundred yards of them; a third soon followed, and the fourth stopped till I got within gun shot, when he retreated, but quite slowly, and appearently very reluctantly. The calf was not dead, but his entrails were partly torn out and he was otherwise so dreadfully lacerated that I went home and fetched my axe and knocked him in the head. Sometimes they will run right through a flock of sheep as they are feeding in the bush, which so frightened them that they scatter in all direction, and creep into the thickets and creeks from whence the shephard has great difficlilty in collecting them, and oftentimes he cannot find them all before night in which case they are all killed before morning. So that one way and the other there is a great number of sheep destroyed by these voracious creatures though there are shephards to attend them by day, and a watchman to guard them by night. There is nothing particular relating to the oppossum beyond what I have told you. The dandicote [bandicoot] is a small animal with a head much resembling a rat and it is not a great deal larger, but quite exempt from the mis-chievous propensity of that vermin: they feed on grass and roots, and their flesh is very delicate food. The wild cats, are of a good size larger than the bandicote; and though the body and tail are somewhat like a cat yet the head more resembles that of a ferret they are pretty numerous, and often do considerable mischief among the poultry on the farms. The dairyman on our farm once found that something skimmed all the cream of his milk round the edges of the ?. This was repeated every night for some time and no place could be discovered were any thing could get in however a trap was set and beated with a piece of new beef and what should be caught but one of these native cats, with a second, a third and a fourth in succeeding nights; and the way they got in we found to be through an underground drain of about 60 yards long the mouth of which had been stopped with a wooden grate, one bar of which was broken leaving just space enough for them to creap in. From this circumstance you will observe that they are cunning little animals: their colour is a black ground, with a number of white spots; and a yallow ground with similer marks of white. The wombut is a very curious animal of a light brown colour with short bow legs and when full ground [grown] is as large as a spaniel dog. The[*y*] seem to have something [*of*] the appearance of a bear but their food is chiefly, if not entirely herba-ceous and as far as ever I heard they are perfectly harmless. We had two young one on our farm for two months or more when one of the[*m*] died, and the other took to the bush. They were very tame and would follow us about the yard but when the first died the other seemed lonly and soon left us. We made surch for him and found him in the head of a tree at no great distance from the farm, from whence he [we] deslodged him and brought him home but he stayed only a day or two before he deserted a second time, and we never saw him afterwords. The squirrel to is a singular animal in size somewhat larger than a hare,, possessing a most beautiful fur of a light colour about the head and shoulders gradually growing darker down the back, till the rump, and its fine large brushy tail is almost black. It have a broad thin flop [flap] on either side uniting with the legs quite down to the talons, which forms no bad substitute for a pair of wings when the creature choose to remove from one tree to another, which it does with the greatest appoint [aplomb] [*and*] ease affording a rather novel scenery in its flight. When resting on a tree the flaps are folded under its belly and are quite imperceptible. Its food is the leaves of trees. The flying fox is of a jet black colour with a fur as soft as velvet and derives its name from the shape of its head and ears, its size a little exceeds that of a mole, and in the article of diet they are not quite so harmless as many others of the animals of that country as the[*y*] come out of the woods by night in considerable numbers into the peach orchards, and nibble the fruit just as mice grow [gnaw] any thing they take a fancy too; and though they eat but little, yet the[*y*] bite hundreds, all of which will rot if nearly ripe, and if green they shibel [shrivel] up, and never come to maturity. I am not aware if they eat other fruit; in fact in a great number of gardens up the country there is but little of other sorts for them. The guano is an animal about four or five feet long, and about as big as the small of a moderate sized person's arm, and in shap exactly resembling a crocodile but in habit not so voracious as that creature, though it is very partial to flesh; and not infrequently incurs the displeasure, and draws forth a volley of curses from the person whole [whose] business it is to attend to the poultry in the farms; for eggs and chicken is its delight Its covering consists of head plates or scales capable of resisting short [shot], so that you might as well do nothing as shoot at them, unless it is when they are up in the trees and you can point the gun at the belly, where the skin is soft and easy penetrated. Its legs are short, and its motion rather slow and awkward on the ground; but it exhibits greater agility in climbing trees; and when once it begins to ascend, I warrant you never set your eye on it, till you see it among the branches, should there be 60 or 70 feet between them and the ground; for if you move [*around*] the tree with your quickest speed, it will always be on the side opposite to were you are. Their bite is not poisonous, but will soon heal. The native mice are a good size larger than our destructive vermin; they are not numerous nor mischievous but live in the bush though I cannot say what they eat. English mice are as numerous, and do as much damage there as they do here but I never saw a rat on any of the farms up the country though the[*y*] literally swarm in Sydney.

Birds

THERE IS A greater variety of these than of beasts, though several of the sorts are not numerous. The following are the most of the kinds that I am acquinted with, the Emu Wild Turkey, Pelican, Eagle, Hawk, three smaller kinds of Hawks, Cockatoos, 7 or 8 different sorts of Parrots, and Parroquets, wild Pigeon, Crane, Wild Duck, Quail, Cuckoo, Magpie, Pluver, Lark, Bellbird, Diamond Sparrow Nankeenbird, Owl, and many others of which I do not know the names one of which is called a Laughing Jackass; it is about the size of a rook, and in plumage not unlike a Jay. They make a noise something like a very hoarse laugh, and it is common for six or eight to get in one tree and thrusting out their heads towards each other, everyone seems to contend for the superiority in the jabbering match which is carried on so that if two persons are never [near] them it is with difficulty they can hear each other speak, so great is the noise produced by those [*word/s missing*] of the forest. They have very large heads and mouth and are of a very uncouth shape altogether; but they are not only a harmless bird, but a useful one; as they will come into the farm yards and catch mice like cats; for which reason many of the settlers are very avirse to having them killed, which some idle fellows will do for sport. They will also kill snakes and eat them; the manner in which they kill them is as follows: they send in the air to a great hight, and then let the snake drop on the hard ground or rock if there is any handy darting down with surprising swiftness, so that they reach the ground almost as soon as the snake and picking it up ascends again and drops it a second time, and sometimes a third, till life is extinct, when they pick it to pieces and devour it. The Emu is a bird of the ostretch kind, and sometimes reaches the hight of six feet; their flesh is good for food, but their chief value consist in the oil which is extracted from them, and which often fetches a very high price. They are hunted with dogs; and so great is the force with which it can kick, that they have been known to kill a dog at a single blow. They are sometimes tamed and kept about gentlemans houses. The wild Turkeys are partly [pretty] numerous in the high mountains parts, and may be seen at times singly, and eight or ten together in some of the settled parts. They are quite as large as the domastic Turkeys, and their flesh as good flavoured. The Pelicans inhabits the sea coast and live chiefly on fish I once saw a great number of them in an arm of the Hunters River when the tribe [tide] was gone out: they were marching through the mud, almost with the regularity of a regiment of soldiers, seemingly in quest of food. In size they are rather larger than a swan, and a great deal longer on the legs. There beak is very sharp, with which they pierce the fish; after having satisfied the cravings of their appetite; this bag when out of use is contracted, and appears to be of small dimensions; but is capable of being extended so that to hold more than two gallons of water, if applied to that purpose. The Eagle Hawk is a large and voracious bird, its size being about on an equality with the Turkey; it have talons of enormous strength and has been frequently [*seen*] to dart on a lamb, and carry it away whole. It is but seldom that you can get near them with a gun, and when you do, it is of no avail to shoot at them unless it be with a bullet, as shot will rattle against them as it will against hard boards and they will fly away as careless as if you had only discharged a popgun at them. Of the other hawks, one is about the size of a sparrow hawk, and the other a size larger than a rook. The latter I never knew to commit any depredations; but the former frequently comes to the farms and borrows a few of the young poultry, as well as prey upon the small birds in the bush. The Cockatoo is a bird to well known here to need that I should discribe it to you; suffice it to say that the[*y*] go in very large flocks, the same as rooks do here and [*are*] extreamly mischievous among the Indian corn, tearing to pieces three times as much as they can eat; and that to with such celerity that in the space of half an hour a flock of them would destroy an acre; so that the settlers are obliged to have a man to watch them constantly; And as their ofice is filled very often by one man, (who is awkward at work) year after year he gains him a name by it, and many of the farms have their Cockatoo Jack, Cockatoo Tom, Cockatoo Dick, and so on. These birds go towards the interior to breed, and I never heard of a nest being found nearer to us than a distance of 40 miles. The largest of the parrots are nearly as big as a rook; and the smallest of the parroquets about the size of a tomtit; and the rest are of various sizes between, and many of them possessing plumage gay and rich in the highest degree. Most of the[*m*] will talk very well talk very well if taken young but those that are caught after they are ful grown will never speak a word. The largest in size is called a king parret, in which the predominating colour is red thoug it possesses many others. The lowery is also very red with a mixture of green and brown about the back and wings. The Green beak is for the most part green with a rich oranged coulered spot on its breast. The rosalla is somewhat larger than a pigeon and its plumage beautiful being variagated with colours of black, blue, green, white, red, yallow, brown, and orange. The blue mountains parrot is a size larger than the rosella and though not possessing such variety of colours yet its fine glossy feathers of orange, red and, blue, are so arranged about its neck and breast, as to give it a most beautiful appearance. They frequently go in large flocks and on a clear morning they glitter in the sun beams like pearls, or diamonds. The cockatoo parrot have a topnot, and is of a greyish colour, and about as large as a thrush, but not very handsom. There is another sort whose name I have forgot, and several and several which I never heard; and all of them in their wild state make a screeching and unpleasant sound. The noise of the parroquets where they are numerous is great, and so shrill that it is quite offensive to the ear. Nearly all the parrotts and parroquets are of migratory habits so that universal stilness pervades the bush (so far as they are concerned) during some months, though there is such a chattering with them at other times. The wild pigeon is about as large as our house pigeons; and I never knew them to be numerous till the last harvest I was there, when they were very plentiful, and I have put up as many as 40 in one piece of wheat stubble. During the five proceding years, four I think was the most I ever saw together. They make tolerable pies [*and*] puddings, but their flesh is very dry. The cock bird have a patch of feathers on each wing of a rich gold colour. The crane I have seen flying at a distance and its neck appear very long, but further than that I know nothing of it. The wild ducks are a little smaller than ours, and their plumage darker; and at times they may be seen in flocks of a dozen but much oftener in pairs. There is a smaller sort that roost in the trees and are called wood ducks. And a larger sort are called shags; these are black, and their flesh is very strong. The quails are not unlike those here, and are very nice eating; but they are far from numerous. The Cuckoo is a large bird at least as large as a rook in the body with a head as big as a moderate sized bason; its mouth is extremely large, and its beak being short, it somewhat resembles a couple of saucers with their concave sides towards each other, and open about an inch on one side. Its voice is very hoarse, and heavy and it never gives vent to a sound after sunrise nor before sunset, but is frequently heard during any of the hours in the night. Its feathers are rather long and loose, and of a dark speckled colour, much resembling women's gouns which I have seen worn for second mournings. There are three sorts of magpies; one black and white all over, and somewhat thicker made than those here; the second is about the same size but much slighter made and shows no colour but black white [while] standing, but when they fly up they exhibit several patchs of white about the wing tail and rump, the third is of a greyish colour all over and is considerably larger than either of the other. The pluver I never saw, though they used to ? ? over from seemingly inconsiderable number by night, and their note is not very different from that of the English pluver. The lark is a little like an English skylark in appearance but widely different as relates to melody; they hop about on the ground but I never saw one ascend in the air; nor make the slightest attempt to sing. The bell bird is a size larger than a sparrow; but I was never near enough to them to observe their colour: there is none of them in the neighbourhood where I resided; but when I was at the Williams River I heard a great many of them in the trees, where they sit and make a noise not much unlike that produced by a sudden twitwh [twitch] of a not very tight wire so that the sound soon dies away but being quickly repeated, and their being a considerable number of birds the bush is kept in a consent [constant] ring by them for an hour or more at a time. The note in my opinion is not very pleasant having too much of a melancholy air belonging to it. The diamond sparrow is a small bird not larger than a robin: its breast and sides are thickly studded with spots of black and white which gives it a very pretty appearance, they are to be seen only about two months in a year about the quarter I lived in. The nankeen bird is as large as a wild duck and the colour of its body corresponds with the name it bears, and its feathers are most beautifully smooth and glassy its neck is of a much lighter colour; out of its pole grows three white feathers almost five inches long which are very Slender, and as soft as velvet and which it can rise up or lay down at pleasure. Altogether it is a very handsom bird. The owl is rather smaller than those here and I never heard it make any noise whatever; its wings are very similar to the screech owl, but its breast, belly, and, sides, are of a white ground full of light black specks not much larger than the head of a pin and both black and white are so very clear that its has a very delecate appearance. There is a small bird called a mutten bird, from its taste when dressed so much resembling the flesh of the sheep. There is a bird (but they are very scarce) which is similar to our thrush in appearance but not in song, for I never heard it attempt to sing. There are several sorts of small birds that I never heard names for; amond which, one is about the size of a tomtit, whose wings and body are of a pale yallow colour mixed with brown; and its head and rump of a bright read; but I think the[*y*] change the latter colour at certain seasons of the year round, and sometimes they were red, and at others they were not. Another sort are much like our water wagtails and so tame that I have known them to fly round my head and strike my hat with their wings. Another sort a little like a hedge sparrow are almost equally tame; or I might omit the "Almost" [W]hien I have been dipping [digging] they have come so close to me to pick up the insects that I have struck them with the spade and several times partially covered them with earth, upon which they would fly up, give a chirp, and dart down again directly. In the district of the Hunter there is a bird called the regeant bird which I heard spoken of as one of the exquisite beauty; but I never saw one of them.

Reptiles

I AM NOT naturilist enough to know exactly what animals are included under this head but snakes at all events are and they are the most formidable enemy to man that the country produces;

not that they will commence an assault, but when struck at, and not wounded they will make a spring at their aggressor; and if he is not dexterous enough to elude it the result might be serious if not fatal. But they are far more dangerous from laying basking in sun among the coarse rough grass in the bush where they are liable to be trodden on without being seen and then they are almost shore to bite. The cattle are very much afraid of them and will in general see them much quicker than a man; and they no sooner set there eye on them they make a speedy retreat. There is a great variety of snakes, and the bite of them is more or less poisioness,—some of them of the most deadly discription [O]ne of those is of a light brown, but which some call a lead colour; and so deliterious is its bite that a person with whom I was acquinted told me that he once saw a dog of his own die from the effect within ten minutes after it was bit. And another man said that he once saw a cow die from the bite in a shorter space than that; the snake biting her in [*the*] side, kept his hold till she fell down dead. They run in general from four to five feet long and proportionably large. The rock snake is considered to be the next worst; they are somewhat smaller of a bright yallow glossy colour and glitter like gold as they glide along in the sunbeams The black snake is the most numerous and in one respect the most dangerous, as the[y] get into the huts, barns, and ricks. My master had a cottage at Westwood, the foundations of which was large trees squared into which the joints for the floors were fixed, which left a hollow space of a foot or more underneath them; and this was a favourite retreat for these black snakes. Some of the boards was laid down when green and having become dry there was large crevices between them though which it was not [*an*] unusual thing to see a snake pop up his head. Sometimes they used to come out to bask in the sun, in which case we frequently killed them. One overseer who was there used to shoot them and a good plan it was for they often lay so close the house that before you could get near enough to strike them with a stick they would find of you and make a speedy retreat. We killed seven there one summer besides what were killed in other parts of the farm. They are about the size and length of a brown snake; black on the back and sides and of a pale pink colour under the belly. Besides these there are some small snakes with dark brown bodies and red heads; whip snakes banded snakes and carpet snakes and [*the*] two latter very large and most beautiful in colour The wip snake is long but very small that is they are not bigger than a persons thum and upwards of a yard in length. Our stockeepers skinned it and the overseer stuffed it with wool and kept it for half a year or more I have seen others from six feet in lingth to seven and a half and proportionately large. The belly is white and black the latter being in small squares and irregularly mixed with the white. Another time he saw a black snake going under the house and caught it by the tail and though unable to draw it back he pulled it in two. The head part lived to the following day and crawled out again but it was very wheak, and unable to make an retreat when he saw myself and another man. There is adders to as some persons afirm but I never saw one and those who say they have differ in their descriptions of them. It is stated that their bite is of so [*word missing*] a nature that either man or beast who comes in contact with their teeth is struck metionless and as sudden as if shot through the body with a musket ball. But from their circumstances of their paucity and the many strange things related of them I have my doubts weather there is such a creature. From the fatal a[*nd*] sudden effects attributed to their bite they are denominated, "death adders" I believe many persons lost their lives from the bite of snakes in the infancy of the Colony; which whet the energies of the scientific, and philanthropic part of the healing medicine. The method resorted to by the blacks when bit by a snake is for a second person to suck the wound, and which they do with such power that in a few minutes the blood will flow copiously from the wound and then they pronounce the patient safe. Of course they are very careful not to swallow any of the poisionous matter. It is seldom however that they can be prevailed on to perform this kind office for a white man; but the latter of which occurred only a short distance from Westwood, and I know both the parties very well. The person bit was a small settler and was ploughing without any shoes when he turned up a snake and stepped on it, who immidiately bit his leg [T]he man that was driving the oxon for him sucked the wound; but weather he did not completely extract that poisionous matter or weather agitation and timedity preyed upon the mind of the man who was bit I cannot say but towards evening he become quite delirious and though he seemed much better the following morning yet at the close of the day his malady returned. This continued three or four days after which no symptoms of derangement appeared, but he was so [*word missing*] in body that he could do little or no work for a fortnight; after which he got quite well. I once trod on a small snake myself; but fortunately my heel come full on its head and crushed it, which prevented him from doing any injury. Lizards abound in most parts of the country; varying in length from three, to eighteen inches, and in size from that of the English oft to four or five inches in circumfrance; but they are all quite harmless. Neither did I ever hear of a snake who proved himself the aggressor; for let them be ever so big, they will make off if they see you in time. The blacks eat them when they kill them themselves, but not otherwise for fear they might have bit themselves, which they often do if wounded, and unable to get away, or reach anything else whereon to take vengeance. Centipedes are very numerous and the bite of them is very poisionous that is persons have been known to loose the joint of a finger from it and when this is not the case, it occasions swelling with the most acute pain, and breaks out into A wound which is sometimes a month in healing. I know a woman who was bit by one of these venemous creatures in the fleshy part of the hand which produced a wound as large as a half crown piece and the flesh decayed till the bone appeared before it began to heal. But the effect is very various on different people, the same as the sting of a bee; some feeling pain without either swelling or wound; some swelling only and some neither one nor the other. The creature when full grown is from three to 6 inches in length with a flat body containing twenty joints, and a pair of legs to every joint so that they have just 40 legs. I have read a discription of the creature either in the

Saturday Magazine or the Visitor (I forget which) where it was stated that the young ones have only a few legs and that they increase as the creature advances towards maturity; but this assertion will not hold good with regards to those in N.S. Wales for I have dug them out of the ground when not much larger than a fine sewing needle and these I found to have 40 legs; and some of these as well as some of the old ones I have brought home with me. The old ones are some of them black, some dark brown, and others of a bluish colour but the young ones, such as I just mentioned are milk white, and lay in a cluster in the ground and the old one with them who will make no attempt to run away when dug up as they do at other times with the greatest speed and will push under the clods or any thing that comes in their way and be out of sight in a moment and when you ? lost sight of them it is a rarity to search after them [I] have found from twelve to twenty young ones with the old one and once twenty seven but being so very small, it is likely that many of them may escape observation among the dirt. They are fond of laying under large stones and among discayed [diseased/decayed] wood in which latter place they are dangerous when one is gathering wood in the bush for [*word missing*]. I see no difference between the common earth worm of north [New] S Wales and that of England only that is [in] the former coutry you will see none at all for many months during droughty seasons. The frogs differ but little of [if] any in shape and size and some of them not a great deal in colour; while others are of a green spotted all over with black. They are frequently to be heard in tops of trees where they making a heavey sort of croaking sort of a noise; but they are more faveourite resort seems to be creek and ponds. Where they suscure [succour] themselves when these are dry I should amagine so from ther noise though it is difficult to see a single one while they are in the water The noise is so srill that it seems to go quite through ones head and at a few yards from a pond when they are in full cry two persons could scarce here each other speak

I must now give you an account of the most pleasent day I experienced in N.S. Wales it was Nov[r.] 19th. 1836, being the sixth anniversary of the commotions for which I was exiled; and on that day I received a little [letter] from England, informing me that a free pardon had been granted me, with permission to return to my native home; and that my fare would be paid by a subscription raised by friends in the neighbourhood where I had lived. We had been reaping oats, and we were just come in to dinner when the dray came from Parramatta, and the man brought me the letter. I opened it and its contents were to me of the greatest delicacies that a palace could afford. I could eat no victuals nor can I describe to you how I felt. I become very anxious to see my name in the Sydney Goverment Gazette; announcing my free pardon; for until it appeared there I could take no steps towards returning to England nor leave the master I was assigned to. There have been instances in which free pardons have been granted to individuals who have been living in the interior and they have been ignorant of the joyful news for as much as two years; but I was not in much danger of being thus cheated; for if my master was inclined to do so, it was now to late as I had become acquainted with the news by letter, and that letter, as if it was so designed by Providence, was directed differently to any I had received before, and came to me without passing through his hands. It was lying at the post office in Parramatta where a person happened to see it who had been at our farm a year or two before, and he very kindly took it out and sent it to me by the man who was at Parramatta with our dray. I once got two other letters in a similar way which I had long been expecting, and when they was brough to me I found wrought on them (by the postmaster I suppose) "Refused by Mr. Macarthur".

Another letter which did come through my masters hands had been broken open, and sealed afresh, as I know by the initials being effaced on the wax; besides, the paper was scorched where it had been held against a candle to melt the wax. Who did this, it is not for me to say, but enough had transpired to create a suspicion in my breast that my liberty might be withheld from me if there was a chance of so doing. So I made it known in the neighbourhood that my pardon had been granted, and those who take the paper promised to let me know as soon as they saw my name there. According on New—years—day 1837 the overseer of Shancomore [*and*] I started for Sydney, where almost my first object was to go to Mr. Walker as my letter directed me to see about a passage home.[25] He told me that a Ship would sail about the 1st. or 2nd. of Feb^ry.^ and if I thought proper I might go in that; and to this I agreed. I next went and got the money (two pounds) which the doctor had put in the Savings Bank at the time of our arrival in the Colony and then I took a place in the Tamer steamer, bound to Maitland on the river Hunter, near to where my brother was living, and a distance of 130 miles from Sydney. The fare was 12s/6d. We sailed out of the harbour about an hour after sunset, and come with[*in*] sight of the lighthouse at Newcastle at daylight the following morning. This is a small town at the mouth of the river, and we sailed in the harbour at 5 o clock and it took five hours to discharge and take in goods, and get a supply of coals and at 10 o clock we proceeded up the river, which I think is as much as much as two miles wide at the town and for a mile above it; but it is anything but a good harbour, the centre of the river is chocked up with mud and the mouth of it rendered very dangerous by sunken [*objects*] the latter being applicable I believe to every navigable river in the country. Right in the centre of the mouth of the river stand [*word missing*] majestic rock, called Nobby's, and which it is conjectured once joined the mainland, but have been seperated therefrom by some awful flood. The banks were not very high and the land for some distance on either side pretty level and altogether the scenery was superial to [*any*] I had witnessed in the country But this I found not to be quite correct for though we had finished our harvest at Westwood a day or two before Christmas I found the people still reaping (Jan[ry.] 5th.) along the margin of the Hunter: and the crop was much inferior to that in the Cowpastures of the same season, but this inferiority was attributable to the drought, which had prevailed to a greater extent on the Hunter than in the Cowpastures that year. I did not consider the land to be better in quality than what I had been used to through [though] there was rather more good sheep land as compared with the hilly tracts than there was where I had been living about. About twenty miles above new castle the Steamer stopped and a and a boat come off from the shore for the mate. There I went on the shore and I had about nine miles to travel through the bush to Branden where my brother was living and I and I believe I should have been rather puzzled to have found my way but fortunl [fortunately] there was a man there who was going to Dungog a farm about two miles from Branden, so I went with him that far, and he directed me the mainder of the way. I found my brother in good health, and no way astonished at seeing me for he had been apprized of the ? over the first hills which lay only a few hundred yards from the river. It is then divided into alternate ranges of hills of moderate height, and swamps at the foot of them; some of which are small and others of great extent. My brother with two of his fellow servants and myself went for a walk the Sunday I was there and we crossed one of these swamps lying between the Williams River and the Pattersons River it measures about one thousand acres and was nearly was cut a mile in length to the Williams River for the purpose of draining it. But it did not seem to answer the end designed, as no part of it was then under cultivation, but was full of great footmarks of cattle which were made in wet weather, and as it was than dry and hard, it was very bad walking. The strips of land on the banks of the rivers is the only portion avaible for tillage in that part of the country for though some of the swamps where originally cleared for agricultural purposes, experience taught the settlers that it would not answer as they are all surrounded by hill from which the water pour in large quantities after a moderate rain and the swamps are innendated for a fortnight, or perhaps a month and the crops of course perish; so that district is chiefly applied to the rearing and and feeding of cattle, but in drought seasons great numbers of them die for want of grass and water, the latter in particular as the rivers are only inlets of the sea and the waters of course as salt as that in the ocean. The cattle are also much annoyed in the swamps by hornets, and other insects. About 20 miles from the mouth of the river a branch turns off to Port Stephens, but without causing any apparent dimination in the principal Stream. Just above this branch I got out of the Steamer and I know nothing of the river above, only that I saw and crossed the Williams River which is another branch from the Hunter. All of them as I said before, are as salt as brine, except for a short time after rain, when the fresh water from the creeks run into them; and after a heavy rain, I have been informed that the water have been found fresh as much as a mile out at sea. I stayed with my brother till the 10th. when he accompanied me through the bush to Reymonds Terrace where we arrived about half an hour before the Steamer came down the river from the Green Hills. As she turned round a bend of the river and came full in our sight, I stepped into a boat that was going to put off to her, and we parted, under the impression that we should meet again that day twelvemonth on the soil that gave us birth, as the public journals of the colony were at that time teeming with extracts from the English papers, which went to show that all those transported for the riots of 1830 were pardoned; and the Sydney Gazzette went so far as to say, that all were to have a free passage home. But though some doubts were entertained as to the passage home, none seemed to exist as to the pardons being granted; for it was stated that Mr. Hume enquired if any thing had been done for the labourers who were banished from the agricultural counties in 1830, when Lord John Russell said, his Majesty had been graciously pleased to pardon them all.[26] Mr. Hume asked, "Were the whole of them pardoned". Lord John Russell replied, "The order makes no distinction". This appeared quite conclusive, and it seemed to give general satisfaction in the Colony and nearly all of the masters who held one of these men, begun bargining with them about wages, not being willing to part with such profitable servants. All now considered themselves free, and the masters did the same, and from this cause my brother and I parted in high spirits, with a confidence as I said before that we should through the favor of Providence soon meet again. The day was very hot, and the water was smooth as glass, so that the vessel glided down the channell with the greatest apparent ease; and the feamale portion of the passengers were remarkably talkative and noisy. But a very different scene [*word obliterated*] presented itself after we had stopped at Newcastle, and sailed again. The wind and the tide were opposed to each other at the mouth of the river which caused the ship [*to*] tumble about considerably, and the women were, one and all very sick and not a word was to be heard from any one of them. We did not reach Sydney till two o'clock in the morning so I remained in the vessell till daylight, and then I went on shore, and again applied to Mr. Walker, to know if the Ship would sail for England, as at first proposed, and he said he believed she would, but if any alteration took place he would write and let me know. So I went up the country again, as it was very expensive living in Sydney, and I was a stranger there with only a small amount of cash. I intended to have come down, a day or two before the ship sailed, but on the 29th. day of Jany. I received a letter from Mr. Walker to say, that the ship would sail on the 26th. This letter had been delayed somewhere, and the day fixed for the vessel's departure being past, I did not attempt to go to Sydney, but wrote again to enquire when the next ship would be ready, and was informed that it would sail on the 6th. or 7th. of March. On the 11th. of February I went to Parramatta for my master, and when there I though the best way would be to go to Sydney (16 miles) and make further enquiries. Mr. Walker said that the time fixed on for the ship's departure remained unaltered, and he advised me to go on board and engage with the captain about my passage to England, which I did; and then proceeded up the country again but before doing which I met a man in Sydney whom I had known up the country; and he very kindly offered me accomodation at his house, if I come down to Sydney again directly. I however stayed at Westwood till the 2nd. of March, when having sent what few things I had by a cart from Vermon[*t*] to Sydney, I followed the next day myself bidding adice [adieu] to my acquaintances, only one whom I expected to see again, and that one, was my shipmate and particular friend Levi Brown, who was in daily expectation of his free pardon; and he much wished me to stay till he received it so that we might come home together; but however much I should have approved of such a companion I could not agree to the proposal, as I had engaged my passage, and was anxious to commence the voyage. I went to Parramatta, and did not reach Sydney till the evening, when I went to the house of my friend and the following morning made enquiries about the ship, (the William Bryan) and I found that she would not sail till the 12th. and when that day arrived a further postponement took place till the 16th. on which day she was positively to sail. But an unforseen circumstance occasioned still further delay. The ships cargo was all in, and on the evening of the 13th. the carpenter was fastening down the hatches when one of those heavy thunderstorms so common in that country came over the town and the lightening struck the main top gallant mast of the William Bryan, and descended to the deck, shivering the yards to splinters, and splitting the mast to its heel. A Board of Survey was held on her the following day, and the upper masts and yards condemned, and the main mast they thought might be repaired; but a second Board of Survey condemned that also. The whole of the repairs occupied till the beginning of April; and as I came to Sydney on the 3rd. of March, I had plenty of time to see a little about the town and I then learned from experience, what I knew before only from hearsay, and such knowledge (as I dare say yourself are aware) is not always of the most satisfactory description; and so it happened in the present instance, for I had been told that clothing was quite as cheap in Sydney as it was in England, and on the strength of this statement in Sydney I frequently went into different shops for some small article, and the owners were always ready every article of clothing was about double the price it is in England. That might be considered the average rate of selling, though some articles are three times as dear as they are here and others not quite double. I have seen shirts sold in Sydney at 4/6, each, as near in quality as I can remember to those I have seen ticketed here at 1/10 and I have seen waistcoats sold at 12/6 which I think would fetch 8/ or 9/ here; though these were disposed of, as I was informed in order to make up a sum of money, the regular selling price being 15/. Weather this was true or not, I cannot say. House rent is very dear. I do not know what the rent of a large house fit for a gentlemans family would be; but a small house with only two rooms, and such as poor men must have if he gets under shelter at all will let for 7/6 a week in the back streets and 10/ if it is in any of the principal streets.

Vegetables are outrageously dear; potatoes sell in general from 10/ to 15/ a cwt and in dry seasons as high as £1. I saw cabbages sold at /10 each that were not much larger than a pint cup when the outside loose leaves were pulled off; and this was not in a dry season. Carrots and other vegitables were equally dear; and all of them are far from good, and it is only in certain spots of the country that they can be grown at all. There is very little fruit of any kind in the market with the exception of peaches, and this I saw offered at a shilling a bushel; while apples were selling at the same time for three pence apiece. Fresh butter sold from 2/6 to 3/ a pound, and salt 1/9 to 2/9; and in very dry times fresh butter have been as high as 5/s a pound. The average price of bacon is from 1/3 to 1/6; cheese the same Tea is mostly to be bought at 2/6 a pound and sugar /6 but the latter is very course. And now for wages; labouring men gets from 18/ to a guinea a week, mechanics 6/ and 7/ a day; and with this sum they are no better off—nay, they are not so well off, as the English workman; for bread is often very dear which I had forgot to mention before. The 2lb loaf was sold as high as tenpence while I was in the country and I understand since I left it, it have been as high as 1/4. But this is not always the case. I have known it as low as /3; and these are the two extremes; about /5 and /6 is a more general price; though it was at /9 and /10 for nearly twelve-months while I was there; and with other articles at the prices I have quoted above. I will leave you to guess how sumptuously the poor men fares in Sydney. I have known goods goods to be seized and sold by auction to pay arrears of rents, more frequently there than here. At least I have known it by advertizements, and hand bills. Before I left the population of Sydney was stated to be 22000, and it was the[*n*] rapidly increasing, both from the arrival of emigrants, and and the number of births in the town.

The town stands, as I think I told you before on land that projects into the sea; and from the extreme point of this projection starts the principal street, George street, so named I imagine from George the third, in whose reign the colony was founded(Jan[y.] 26th. 1788) This street is upwards of a mile in length; I should think a mile and a half, and contains some very handsom shops, and elegant buildings are of brick, but very few of that material have been put up for some years, as stone is now chiefly used, of which there is an almost inexhaustible store.

Many of the buildings in George street, are equal in beauty to almost any in London; and there are not more than half a dozen weatherboarded houses in that street, which so much disfigure other parts of the town. But there is a long dead wall against the military parade ground which quite spoils that part of the street. From the projection point where George street commences, the land widens very fast and soon forms space for parallel streets which on the eastern side of George street, are named after the numbers [members] of the royal family, and two of them on the west side after two of the Ministers of State. The streets on the E. side are York, Kent, Cumberland and Sussex; and on the W. side Pitt, Castlerigh, Elizebath, and Philip. The last named street it is named after the first Governor of the Colony but why the name of Elizabeth was given to a street lying between that, and those called after the Ministers of State I never heard. On the E. side of George street, the Military barracks and the parade ground, forming a large square, is very detrimental to the good management of the town, as it completely dissevers York and Kent streets; and strong hopes were entertained before I left the country that Goverment would sell it, for building on, and errect barracks outside the town; and if they do so it would be advisable to go a good distance back for the present barracks were outside the town when they were built. And so was the old burial ground which had been walled round and shut up nearly twenty years before I came away; and at the expiration of that period I believe it was proposed to throw it open and build on it. It is situated at the edge of what is still called the Brickfields, that is, where bricks were made for the use of the town but which fields are now covered with houses and a number of streets run across each other from N & S. and from east & west and ? more than half range from the old to the new burying ground, which are about a mile asunder. This part of the town was sadly disfigured, and a great many houses rendered untenable at the time I left from the following cause. George Street extended through these fields, and down a rather steep Hill called Brickfield Hill, and the Goverment took it into their heads to employ an iron gang in lowering this hill. The deepest part of the cut was twelve or fourteen feet, and the houses were left standing on a bank that much above the leval of the street; and as the earth that was taken from the hill was used in filling up the valley, the houses in that part were subjected to an equal inconvenience though of a different character, for their first story was quite beneath the level of the new made street. Some persons who had houses on the hill were pulling them down, and others I observed proping them up while they dug the earth out from under them, and formed another story; a rather novel way of building you will think, to form the bottom last, but such I saw in progress. The cross streets were rendered useless for anything but foot persons, as they terminated abruptly with a precipice on either side when they came to George Street; but these cross streets, as well as one or two others running parallel with George Street, were to undergo a like process of lowering, and some of them were partly done. Several accidents had happened, and two or three persons were seriously injured by falling down the precipices and great complaints were made at the streets being left in such a condition to endanger the limbs and probably the lives of the inhabitants. There are a great many cross streets, that go by the names of the of the Governors who have administred the affairs of the Colony, and others are named after the Secretaries, and Colonels, and Mayors who have been there. About a mile or a mile and a half out of the town is some eleveled [elevated] land called the Surrey Hills were there are many neat buildings, and in the depressions between the hills is the best gardens I saw in the Colony. From these hills there is a good view of that broad expance of water called Botney Bay, which is five or six miles by land, and ten by water from Sydney, and is the site originally fixed on for the formation of the Colony; but Governor Philip finding the land about it low, and the harbour distitute of shelter, fixed upon Port Jackson and laid the foundation of Sydney, which have now grown in[*to*] a populous city; and which during the half century of its existance have I suppose been the theatre of more moral turpitude than any other spot on the face of the earth. There are I believe a few of the "First fleeters" as they are called still living in the Colony, and to them (in spite of the reigning demoralization) it cannot but be a matter of interest to reflect on what the hand of industry, but more the compulsory labour of exiles have done. What must they feel when they consider the time that Nature reigned the sole monarch of that vast continent, and see it now when the hand of civilization have made such inroads upon her forests. They, or many of them perhaps may feel uninterested in witnessing the change; but for my part I felt what I cannot express when I beheld streets thronged with inhabitants buildings of the most magnificent discription and crowded markets, with several large steamer flour mills; and then look back in imagination fifty years, and see that spot a desolate wilderness; and again, to see the harbour studded with merchant ships over whose waters, most probably, before that time, a sail had never been spread.

Epilogue

'Our worldly prospects are gloomy'

JOSEPH ARRIVED BACK in England in the second half of 1837 and was writing his account in February 1838. Whether he returned briefly to Bullington and the Dever Valley is not known, but it seems unlikely. He no longer had his smallholding and with his political reputation he would have had difficulty in finding work as a labourer anywhere in the area. By 1839 he had settled his family about 20 miles from Bullington at Brunswick Place, off the Bath Road, in Reading in Berkshire. He was still there in 1841 at the time of the census. On the birth certificates of his children, born in 1839 and 1841, Joseph recorded his occupation as 'labourer'. It is evident that he was no less energetic or prudent than he had been before his transportation, because by 1851 he had established himself as a small tenant farmer at Winnersh, near Wokingham. Between 1838 and 1848 the Chartist movement revived the claim of working men to have the vote. While it is highly likely that Joseph sympathised with a political agenda which was so similar his own he cannot, as yet, be linked to Chartism in Reading.

Moors Farm, in the parish of Hurst, was only 26 acres. Although Joseph must have sold enough produce and livestock to pay his rent and taxes, he is probably best described as a peasant or yeoman, farming chiefly to maintain his family. He grew a few acres of cereals, some root crops and garden vegetables, kept a cow or two, fattened pigs occasionally and fed a horse and poultry. For around ten years Moors Farm sustained the five members of the Mason family but it was, according to Joseph's own reckoning, a 'hand to mouth' existence and the precarious family economy was easily upset. In 1860 the potatoes were badly blighted and the wet, cold summer ruined the other root crops, delayed the harvest and spoiled the wheat. Joseph's worries were further compounded by the death of a horse which had cost him £15, followed by that of a pig worth £1 and two calves. Although he survived that crisis, he was unable to survive another in 1861. He had acquired a mare and got her in foal in the hope that he would thus have working horses for as long as he continued at Moors Farm. The death of both animals ended his hopes; he wrote that it 'completely breaks us down . . . we shall be under the necessity of leaving the farm . . . and altogether our worldly prospects are gloomy'. In October 1861 he was forced to sell up. He realised £52 from his livestock and less than £50 from his crops after he had paid his tithes, rent and rates.

Joseph's health was increasingly poor; he talked of himself as a virtual cripple fit only for a job as a copying clerk—if he could find such a position. He had written to Robert and told him of the dreadful pain in his swollen legs and how, when writing his letters, he had to raise his legs upon a chair. He was, therefore, grateful for the kindness of the neighbouring farmer who bought Moors Farm and allowed him to stay on in the house and do little jobs around the place on a salary of £20 a year while Ann looked after the poultry. When Joseph died at Moors Farm on 3 October 1863, he was severely incapacitated by oedema, probably due to congestive cardiac failure. His death did not surprise Robert who commented that 'when the legs thus give way one's earthly pilgrimage is nearly at an end', but he very much regretted that he had not seen Joseph since they had parted at Raymond Terrace in January 1837. For years the brothers had kept up a vigorous, informed and detailed correspondence about family matters and local, national and international affairs. Letters and newspapers were posted in both directions and plans were always being developed for Robert's visit home.

When he finally returned for a visit in 1864, Robert was disappointed with England. He felt ill at ease and out of place after thirty-three years in New South Wales, but his greatest sorrow was that he had not returned sooner. Joseph had been the person he most wanted to see and his absence created 'a vast void'. Death separated these brother-radicals, brother-protesters and brothers-in-exile, but through the fortuitous survival of his memoir Joseph Mason speaks to us today from the 'vast void' that is our past.

David Kent

Endnotes

[1] A total of 146 men were transported to New South Wales for their part in the Swing disturbances of 1830–31. Their county of origin was as follows: Hampshire 49, Berkshire 40, Wiltshire 36, Dorset 13, Bedfordshire 2, and one each from Cambridgeshire, Derbyshire, Herefordshire, Kent, Norfolk and Shropshire.

[2] Simonstown, a settlement on the eastern side on the peninsula which terminates in the Cape of Good Hope, offered a more sheltered harbour in False Bay than was available at Cape Town on the Atlantic coast about 12 miles distant.

[3] The route across the southern ocean known in maritime circles as the Great Circle used the westerly winds of the 'Roaring Forties'.

[4] This would seem to be a reference to Psalm 107: 25–26.

[5] Hannibal Macarthur, nephew of John Macarthur, lived at Vineyard Cottage, a short distance from Parramatta. Mason passed most of his sentence at Westwood, Macarthur's property on the Nepean River.

[6] There was nothing unusual in Mason worshipping at both the Methodist chapel and the Anglican church. Although by 1831 the Methodists had existed as a separate denomination for nearly fifty years, John Wesley believed that his followers should remain within the Church of England. For someone like Mason, a Low Churchman, a devout believer and political radical, Methodist religious practice was very appealing. Methodism stressed the equality of man. Its forms of worship were simple and musical, and it was the denomination of the common people while Anglicanism, the official creed, was the religion of the masters.

[7] In fact Edmund Lockyer only arrived in the colony in 1825.

[8] Robert Mason was assigned to Major Benjamin Sullivan, the Resident Magistrate at Port Macquarie, but Branden, the property where he was sent to work, was situated near Dungog on the east bank of the Williams River which joins the Hunter River above Newcastle.

[9] The rations allowed to convict workers provided a far better diet than labouring men could expect in southern England where rural labourers rarely tasted meat.

[10] Shancomore, established by J. T. Campbell on land granted by Macquarie, was situated at the junction of the Bringelly Creek with the Nepean River in the County of Cumberland.

[11] John Manning, appointed as the Registrar of the Supreme Court of New South Wales in 1828, leased Vermont from W. C. Wentworth. The property was situated to the south of Shancomore on the other side of the Bringelly Creek and was opposite Westwood across the Nepean.

[12] Thomas Shepherd was a pioneer nurseryman in Sydney. Contrary to the prevailing fashion he recommended the use of native plants in colonial gardens. His ideas were widely disseminated by the publication in 1836 of his *Lectures on Landscape Gardening in Australia*.

[13] The crossing is marked on modern maps as Campbell's Ford.

[14] The pool is known today as Bents Basin.

[15] Montpellier was established by William Panton in 1824 on a grant of 2000 acres taken up at Stonequarry near Picton. Mason was visiting John Burroughs who had been convicted of demanding money from a farmer at Ebbesbourne Wake in Wiltshire. His death sentence had been commuted to 14 years transportation. Burroughs was assigned to Panton who in 1834 described him as 'in every respect a good and useful member of the community'. Burroughs and Levi Brown (see footnote 17) hailed from neighbouring villages and almost certainly knew each other.

[16] The act, 11 Geo. IV No. 8, was passed in 1830 and extended for another three years in 1832.

[17] Levi Brown, aged 38, a thatcher and agricultural labourer from Broad Chalk in Wiltshire, was convicted at the Special Commission in Salisbury of demanding money with menaces and destroying a chaff-cutting machine. His death sentence was commuted to 14 years transportation. Brown was a hard-working, respectable man. According to the farmers of the parish who got up a petition in the hope of reducing the severity of his sentence he was always a 'steady, quiet and well-behaved man'. He was assigned to J. E. Manning at Vermont.

[18] This portion of the text is not in Joseph Mason's handwriting. To make sense it should read as either 'from blacksmith George' or 'from a blacksmith's forge'. On balance we think the latter is more likely. The confusion probably arises from the mistakes which inevitably occur when one person is writing to the dictation of another.

[19] It has proved impossible to identify the source to which Mason alludes.

[20] Scall is a scaly eruption on the skin and the complaint to which Mason refers was probably either dry scall, an irritation caused by the itch-mite, or moist scall, a form of eczema.

[21] The Native Institution was established by Governor Macquarie in 1814. Contrary to Mason's claim, there were very few legal marriages between aboriginal women and white men although there were numerous instances of cohabitation. The authorities did not offer inducements to persuade white men to take aboriginal brides and Mason probably misunderstood the nature of the grants made to ticket-of-leave men, some of whom lived with native women.

[22] The mission at Wellington Valley was established in 1832 but the court case to which Mason refers arose from remarks J. D. Lang made in 1836 about Lancelot Threlkeld's management of the Lake Macquarie Mission. Threlkeld was successful in his suit but instead of the one thousand pounds which he sought he received a qualified apology and damages of one farthing.

[23] The incident to which Mason refers was probably the 'Appin Massacre' of 1816 which occurred during Governor Macquarie's campaign against the Aborigines of the Cumberland Plain.

[24] In 1829 Governor Darling attempted to stop uncontrolled expansion by discouraging settlement beyond the regions which had been officially surveyed. This policy was not effective and in 1835 Governor Burke legalised the situation by granting grazing rights to squatters on payment of a licence fee.

[25] Mason was probably instructed to approach Walker Bros. and Co., merchants and shipping agents. Operated by Thomas and William Walker the company exported large amounts of wool to London during the late 1830s.

[26] Joseph Hume was for many years the leading radical Parliamentarian. Lord John Russell was Home Secretary and leader of the Commons in the Whig ministry from 1835–41. The Swing protesters undoubtedly benefited from the public outrage which followed the prosecution and transportation of the Tolpuddle martyrs in 1834 and resulted in their pardon in 1836.

Tomah
K. Geo. Mt
Mt Hay
Grose R.
Richmond
Common
The Highlands
Small Settlers
Castlereagh
Black Heath
Govetts Leap
Pulpit Hill
64
Weatherboard Hut
K
The Blue Mountain
Kings Table Land
Twenty mile Hollow
51
Springwood
43
Shepherd
Lord
King
Penrith
Emu
Woodriffe
Tindall
W. Cox
J. Norton
Mulgoa C.
Cosgrove
Jamisons Valley
Govetts Point
Wentworth
J. Blaxland
Bunn
Palmer
Blaxland
Campbell
Lowe
Farrel
Coxes R.
Warragamba R.
Cobbity
N
D
Vanderville
Inglis
Florence
Oakes
Church
Reserve
Carbon
Howe
Baloon
Tonalli
Colong
Red Brook